DOMESTIC ART

© 2008 Assouline Publishing
601 West 26th Street, 18th floor
New York, NY 10001, USA
Tel.: 212 989-6810   Fax: 212 647-0005
www.assouline.com

© 2008 PaperCity magazine

Printed in China

ISBN: 978 2 75940 303 5

PRINCIPAL PHOTOGRAPHY BY KA YEUNG AND TRIA GIOVAN

ADDITIONAL PHOTOGRAPHY BY STEVE WRUBEL, STEPHEN KARLISCH,
GUILLAUME GARRIGUE, JACK THOMPSON, PAUL HESTER, HICKEY-ROBERTSON AND MALI AZIMA

DOMESTIC ART

CURATED INTERIORS

HOLLY MOORE

ROB BRINKLEY   **LAURANN CLARIDGE**

ASSOULINE

CONTENTS

INTRODUCTION

There have been periodicals throughout time that capture a unique mind-set, that pique a curiosity to look at things anew, appreciate oddities, and revel in uniqueness and personal work. That's what *PaperCity* magazine has become—a loopy but sublime drawing-room comedy featuring dandies and soulful poets, fashion directors and style aesthetes . . . all lounging, sipping, and chattering away in 18th-century châteaux inserted into downtown lofts, whitewashed shotgun houses filled with Twomblys and Rauschenbergs, and dark-as-a-hedgehog tiny Tudors.

So just why is *PaperCity* irrationally known throughout the States, even though it's published solely in Dallas and Houston? We haven't a clue. But we do know it's the home-design pages that have captured the more—shall we say—delicious detritus of decorating. The selected houses in this book were pulled from the pages of *PaperCity*, from the years 2000 to 2008—roughly a decade of design alchemy and clinking highballs. We foraged for both the musty and gutsy and the soaring and sensual, from a five hundred-square-foot bedsit to a Philip Johnson architectural wonder. The fact that these interiors all happen to be in Texas is *very* curious in itself, and would probably take too much psychological babble to interpret. We think it's the fact that there is so much space—so much *air*—in Texas that inspiring design just ferments.

I, along with arguably the two most design-obsessed editors at *PaperCity*, Rob Brinkley and Laurann Claridge, have curated thirty-seven glorious projects, from follies to disciplined mansions, from Dominique and John de Menil's International-style house with its interior by the great couturier Charles James to artist Christian Eckart's abandoned 1940s warehouses polished to gleaming architectural wonder. Marvel at a compound of rescued, early-1900s clapboards and an 1880s German-immigrant cottage inhabited by art dealer Hiram Butler. We've included a '50s masterwork by the great organic architect Bruce Goff and a collected ode to glamour by Ken Downing and Sam Saladino. George Sellers' industrial space crackles with his own surreal designs, while designer Michael Landrum's chalet-style 1913 bungalow manifests the best bits and pieces of the past. Artist McKay Otto's turn-of-the-century seaside gingerbread is a study in anthropology peppered with good art; antiquarian Eric Prokesh aims his cerebral arrows at Louis this and Louis that, then electrifies it all with saturated color; and decorator Michelle Nussbaumer installs an eighteenth-century château *and* an old-world hunting lodge in one downtown loft space. Meanwhile, art director Mike Thompson sips Scotch neat in his Scotch Room, watched over by two mounted deer, a pheasant and a wildebeest.

Shouldn't everyone have a wildebeest . . . and a Scotch Room?

— Holly Moore Kastleman, May 2008

MIKE THOMPSON

He looks a bit like a soulful poet who took a slight left down Carnaby Street. He loves all things shiny and fabulous but bangs around town in an old green pickup truck. He's got the acerbic wit of Truman Capote, but it's cut with homespun humbleness. And the place where he lives? Well, frankly, that's where all these personalities come crashing together.

Welcome to Mike Thompson's pad: salon of the good story, showcase of Scotch, experimental lab for a virtuoso of the vignette. It's all in a day's work for this interior decorator, television-commercial art director, and event stylist. Indeed, Thompson spins his visual magic for the small screen and the big soirée: You think he could resist *not* perfecting his craft at home? Witness the two taxidermy birds that dangle from a cabinet latch. The button-tufted midcentury bench whose animal-like legs crouch on a zebra-print carpet. The wildebeest that watches over a collection of crystal decanters in the Scotch Room. Wildebeest? Scotch Room? Kindly note: Thompson is the sort who would find it strange that you *don't* have a wildebeest.

Oh, to be given an empty room. Several empty rooms. That was the titillating conundrum facing Thompson when he found this house—a solid-brick, 1938 classic American duplex—about three years ago. He saw multiple opportunities for his display urges. "I *love* lots of little rooms," he says, eyes sparkling behind his trademark glasses. The thing is, Thompson already had enough furniture, props, rugs, and art to fill fifteen houses, maybe more. (All part of his professions, you see.) Thinking that the new space looked rather cavernous, so empty and all, he did what any diehard hunter-gatherer would do. "I went on a big, giant shopping spree." He pauses to laugh out loud. "But I filled it with the new before I ever got to fill it with the old!" Now, "new" to Thompson could mean all sorts of things: a weathered "Bird Hous" sign (the "e" went missing long ago) from a zoo; a pop-art mobile bought from an artist in Fort Worth; even remnants of the patterned carpets he has specified for various charity luncheons. But not everything was snapped up in an adrenaline-fueled frenzy. He sweetly mixes in a colonial spindle bed that was once his godmother's and pieces of Rosenthal-Nutter pottery that were his family's. Indeed, he confirms, he was one of those kids who always collected, always curated. As he says this, two mounted deer and the wildebeest peer from behind. Everywhere there are abstract prints, oil paintings, and animal horns. Not one surface unadorned. "Oh," he says, resolutely, "I was the *hoarder*."

opposite In Mike Thompson's unforgettable Scotch Room, a wildebeest and friends watch over a collection of vintage Scotch decanters and a beautifully battered Chesterfield chair. The art was drawn from a manic mix of sources, from estate sales to a Neiman Marcus prop sale.

preceding pages Mike Thompson's no-holds-barred bedroom features a Colonial bed wearing a llama blanket. Over the bed is a painting by Matt Williams, at far right is a large figurative painting bought for $70. *opposite above* In Thompson's "Scotch Room" the amber elixir is kept, ever-ready, in vintage decanters. An 1800s bust fronts an estate-sale oil painting that Thompson crowned with antlers. The brass bar trolley is 1970s, as is the zigzag chrome shelf beyond the red-leather Chesterfield chair. *opposite bottom left* Taxidermy birds. *opposite bottom right* A detail of the sitting room. The mix of art is 1960s-estate-sale, contemporary, and even Thompson's own work, upper left. *above* The sitting room is a heady mix of Florence Knoll club chairs, a pillow-festooned Chesterfield sofa, and an antique mirror flanked by a pair of birds from England, won on eBay. The large abstract painting is by Kirsten Macy. *right* More taxidermy friends. *following pages* The luxe living room is spun as part library, part design museum. The carpet is left over from an Etro charity event that Thompson decorated. The mobile is by a Fort Worth artist; the fluorescent-tube work, far right, is Thompson's own. "I made myself a Dan Flavin," he says.

DOMINIQUE and JOHN DE MENIL

A house is not always just a house. In the instance of Dominique and John de Menil, their International-style home in Houston, Texas—completed in 1951 by architect Philip Johnson and decorated by legendary couturier Charles James—teetered on the edge of the avant-garde. It was the first private home that Johnson, a disciple of minimalist Ludwig Mies van der Rohe, was commissioned to design, and the result shocked many of the affluent neighbors ensconced in their châteaus and mock-Tudor manses. They didn't know what to make of its flat roof, plain brick facade and lack of manicured landscaping—plus, it scandalously faced a roadway once used primarily by the neighborhood's servants.

One would have to look to Dominique de Menil for answers. An unpretentious woman who possessed an unself-conscious beauty, Dominique harbored a curious intellect and a contemplative nature. Her husband, Jean (who would later anglicize his name to John), was a decorated French soldier and former banker who joined and later became chairman of Schlumberger, an electronics company specializing in oil-exploration equipment founded in France by Dominique's father and uncle. A member of the French Resistance, John was born into a titled French Catholic family of modest means yet had the will—along with his equally high-minded wife—to change society.

In a pivotal event that would alter the course of their lives, the de Menils were introduced to modern art by the Dominican priest Father Marie-Alain Couturier. On a quest to find a place for the burgeoning modern-art movement in the Catholic Church, Couturier would come to commission buildings such as Le Corbusier's famous chapel in Ronchamp and the Henri Matisse chapel in Vence. He acquired the work of Georges Braque, Marc Chagall, Fernand Léger, and others for the churches of Audincourt and Assy in France. His passion for art was infectious. Soon after the de Menils befriended him, they began a lifelong journey of their own, collecting works by Braque, Léger, Henri Matisse, Pablo Picasso, and postwar artists Joseph Cornell, Jasper Johns, Barnett Newman, Robert Rauschenberg, Mark Rothko, and Andy Warhol. In total, they acquired one of the world's largest collections of the surrealist works of Max Ernst and René Magritte, Byzantine and medieval art, and a cache of the native art of Africa, Oceania and the Pacific Northwest. Their zeal for collecting culminated in the acquisition of more than 15,000 pieces and the eventual founding of The Menil Collection, the world-renowned Houston museum opened in 1987 by the steel-willed Dominique, the widow who survived her husband by more than twenty years.

But before there was The Menil Collection, there was the de Menil house, the modernist Johnson structure that was home for five decades not only to the ever-expanding stash of art collected by

opposite In the Magritte room, formerly Dominique de Menil's bedroom, hangs *The Origins of Language* by René Magritte, one of three works by the surrealist in this room. Artwork © 2008 C. Herscovici, London/Artist Rights Society (ARS), New York. Below it are a pair of neoclassical Italian walnut side chairs and a Louis XV provincial-style worktable made of beechwood, circa 1770.

opposite In the living room, the steel-gray wall is an early version of what is known as Menil gray. The painting is titled *Return of the Beautiful Gardener* by Max Ernst. Artwork © 2008 Artists Rights Society (ARS), New York/ADAGP, Paris. Dominique de Menil and her daughter Christophe designed the seven-sided ottoman, while the bluish-gray chaise longue is the work of couturier Charles James. **above** The de Menils in 1968. **below** The restored Philip Johnson–designed home, completed in 1951.

the de Menils, but also to the couple and their five children. Upon the death of Dominique, at age eighty-nine in 1997, the home was bequeathed to the Menil Foundation. In 2001, the foundation undertook an ambitious three-year preservation and conservation project, led by William F. Stern and David Bucek of Stern and Bucek Architects in Houston, to return the 5,600-square-foot house to the way it had appeared when the de Menils had first furnished it. Essentially, the interior had remained unchanged, with the exception of art that rotated in and out. But after fifty years, like most structures, a bit of spiffing up was in order.

The house is set back from the street on three lush acres, its borders marked with a towering thicket of bamboo. The story goes that the recent émigrés, unsure in the late '40s about the financial security of Schlumberger or their life in the States, told Johnson they wanted to situate the one-story house on the property in such a manner that if they needed to sell off a parcel of the land, they could— hence, the decision to place the house in the center of the acreage with huge expanses of greenery in the front and back. The entrance is essentially a blank facade, while the house's salmon-hued brick walls seem to measure to infinity, interrupted only by a very un-Miesian anomaly: four windows, probably requested by the clients, added to the kitchen.

The rooms are organized around the courtyard, and in the original plans there was no dining room. Well, there was, but it was called the playroom. Armed with strong opinions, the de Menils were never shy about expressing them. In a letter to Johnson, Dominique notes, "We want the entry to be large enough to set a dining table in." Thus, in the foyer, there is room enough to accommodate several tables of twelve, as well as a floor-to-ceiling, blue-and-white Yves Klein canvas. Here, Dominique and John entertained at dinner parties honoring artists such as Magritte, Henri Cartier-Bresson, and Ernst, as well as internationally known scholars, visiting filmmakers such as Roberto Rossellini and Jean-Luc Godard, and liberal-minded political leaders and activists in the civil-rights movement of the '60s and '70s—a cause that often made the vocal de Menils locally unpopular.

When the subject of decorating her house came up, Dominique said in a recorded interview, "We know what Philip would have done; it would have been very modern furniture, something expected." But the de Menils took everyone by surprise—especially Johnson—when they hired couturier Charles James to fashion the interior. James was a temperamental fashion designer with perfectionist tendencies and peculiar work habits. At the urging of her husband, Dominique—and, later, her eldest daughter, Christophe—became clients, commissioning James to create sculptural, beautiful, timeless couture gowns and suits. Today, those gowns are still done up in their Charles James boxes and ribbons, off-view in the "treasure rooms" of the Menil museum.

In what is believed to be the only residential interior he ever designed, James insisted that the original low ceilings (typical of the International style) be raised ten inches, to the displeasure of Johnson. Within the ever-changing, art-filled walls of the sharp-edged house, James included pops

opposite In Dominique de Menil's dressing room, Charles James applied a brushed-paint treatment on the wardrobe doors in an array of grayed pastels that has survived decades without repainting. A game table doubles as a dressing table. Behind it is one of a pair of American Rococo-revival laminated rosewood side chairs in the style of John Henry Belter, circa 1850.

opposite The makings for cocktails are tucked away in this walk-in drinks closet, along with taxidermy birds and a collection of miniature works by artists from Marc Chagall to Jean Hugo. Notice the curvy shelves and the original felt-covered door, both signature Charles James touches. **above left** Dominique de Menil's modest bath was tucked away behind this strangely sumptuous red velvet curtain. The ceramic phrenology head is nineteenth-century English. The Directoire-style fruitwood chest is Austrian Biedermeier, circa 1810. The mask is an early twentieth-century piece from South Guinea. **above right** The nineteenth-century pine armoire with carved, cutout panels is believed to be Mexican. Above it hangs René Magritte's oil-on-canvas *Force of Circumstance*. **right** Mimicking a funhouse effect, Charles James covered myriad doors in the children's wing with mirrors, lush antique red velvet, and fun pops of hot-pink felt. The wool carpet in mustard and baby-blue hues adds even more interest to the color play.

above An embossed-leather screen separates this sitting room from the hall. Charles James designed the curvaceous, wool-covered Lipstick sofa in the early 1950s. Mid-nineteenth-century American laminated rosewood slipper chairs, in the manner of John Henry Belter, surround an oval Circassian-walnut cocktail table with wrought-iron legs constructed by the artist Jim Love and designed by Dominique de Menil. The Max Ernst portrait of Mrs. de Menil, 1934, was the first important art commissioned by the de Menils. *below left* In the foyer is a jade-green, raw-silk-covered Venetian rococo settee made of walnut, circa 1755 to 1765. *below right* In Mrs. de Menil's bedroom, a pair of timeworn eighteenth-century Italian walnut open armchairs, covered in cut velvet, flanks a round pedestal table. The crucifix is from the Republic of the Congo and Angola and once hung above Mrs. de Menil's bed. A Giacometti-designed standing Minerva lamp, circa 1935, is at right.

of luscious color, sensual Rococo-style furniture, and custom-upholstered pieces of his own design. Arriving at the house just as workers were headed to lunch, James often labored late into the night, even employing young Christophe and her sister, Adelaide, to hold up lights and cardboard cutouts the scale of intended furnishings. Never straying far from his penchant for dressmaker fabrics and textiles, James used plush antique silk-velvets and humble wool felt dyed in rich ochre, subtle gray, and deep rose-petal hues to line the backs of doors, upholster niches, and create an optical play off the mirrored doors in the corridor of the children's wing.

Elizabeth Ann Coleman, a Charles James scholar who curated the seminal retrospective of his work in 1982 at the Brooklyn Museum of Art, was brought in to assess which pieces needed to be repaired and which should simply remain as they were. Most painted or fabric-covered walls, niches, and doors in good condition were deemed "sacred" by the conservation team and left untouched, protected from the debris and hazards of construction by false walls built around them. Elizabeth Lunning, the chief conservator at The Menil Collection, recalls, "When I came out here with Ann Coleman, she was saying that Charles James was always picking up used fabrics. One thing everybody who sees these velvet-covered doors in the children's wing says is, 'Why is there a seam down the middle?' She thinks it's very possible that it had a seam down the middle when James bought it."

Sacred, too, was a drinks closet off the living room, festooned with miniature paintings by artists in the Menils' collection and shelves of barware—a mix of dime-store glasses and finer cocktail accoutrements. Perched on the shallow shelves: a half-dozen taxidermy birds that met their demise when they smacked into the expansive windows lining the back of the house. Also sacrosanct were the floor-to-ceiling bookcases in the hallway, with a rolling library ladder, that housed John's philosophy books, French literature, and art catalogues raisonnés. The Menil conservation department was careful to remove and then replace each book after construction was completed, just as they had found them.

To the consternation of the conservation team, a firm hired to analyze the house's original paint treatments revealed that "James wanted to use very lush colors, but at the time you couldn't go to Benjamin Moore ... and find them, so he hand-mixed a lot of these colors," Lunning says. "If you look around on the walls close enough, there are variations on the color. He might have put up a color and, if he didn't like it, [he'd] change it midway."

Today the preserved midcentury house may serve many functions: an archive or a space to hold special events and lectures. Yet one use this house will never serve, as mandated by the foundation and the de Menil heirs, is that of house-museum. "The de Menils were very independent in the way they saw and combined and lived with art," the Menil director Josef Helfenstein says. "To them it was very spiritual and intuitive. And that is very palpable in their home today." And although it may be impossible to recreate the magical aura that once filled this house, for the lucky few who now walk through its fabled rooms and view the priceless, changing display of art, it feels—as the preservation team intended—as if the de Menils might walk through the doors at any moment and invite you to stay for a nice long chat about Magritte.

CHRISTIAN ECKART AND JILL DAVIES

Few driving by this dicey neighborhood would pick out a pair of failing warehouses as likely structures for a sleek, contemporary living space. Today's gleaming home and studio for international artist Christian Eckart and his wife, Jill Davies, prove that even the most unlikely architectural transformations are possible, fueled by imagination, inspiration, and a finely tuned technical prowess.

Christian Eckart and Jill Davies typify a thoroughly international couple. Both Canadian by birth, they met in Brooklyn when he was living and traveling between his base there and European culture capitals Berlin and Amsterdam, carving out an acclaimed international art reputation with polished, monochromatic aluminum-and-lacquered abstractions that manifest equal parts painting and sculpture. Lured to Houston, Texas, in part by longtime dealers Robert McClain and Cynthia Cage McClain, Eckart exhibits at their gallery and recently taught at the Glassell School of Art.

Eckart and Davies spotted but initially rejected the derelict, abandoned 1940s- and 1960s-era adjoining warehouses. Yet somehow the couple kept circling back to them before taking the plunge into a bold domestic project. Eckart's precise, unerring artistic aesthetic came into play as he served as spatial designer, following early advice from an architect acquaintance. "This was an extreme renovation," reflects Davies. "We maintained the structural steel but redid the envelope and the interior buildout. We kept the pads but poured another four inches and had the floors done as a sub-floor with the bamboo. Technically it was very difficult." Eckart adds, "I became a living blueprint and literally hand-drew the master suite and Jill's bathroom, closet, and exercise suite."

The finished minimal nest has exquisitely honed details, executed with a precisionist vigor by an artist who is accustomed to working with industrial fabricators, employing measurements down to the nearest centimeter. From the straightforward portal with industrial doors to the expansive, high-ceilinged interiors, the space is home to a carefully considered collection of artworks by contemporaries (and often friends), as well as a trove of art books and Asian antiquities, the latter taking up residence in a blue Formica display case that looks like an oversized Donald Judd sculpture. Everywhere, the coolness of minimalism has been warmed by the golden tones of bamboo flooring, natural light washing in from skylights and ten-foot-high windows off the dining area, and the pure, reflective glow of Eckart's nonobjective art. The complex not only serves as a domestic dwelling but also as an artist studio. Eckart's actual working space is in a compact room upstairs in the 1940s-era north building, where he sketches, reads, and envisions his next projects.

opposite In the living room is Mark Flood's painting of Marilyn Monroe. The American- and German-made audio equipment, which Eckart calls "my boom box," was purchased piece by piece online. The concrete bench was designed by the artist.

opposite top The living room is punctuated by Eckart's monumental *Sacra Conversazione* paintings, dated 1988 to 2002, one of his best-known series. The circa-1960s coffee table is a find from a flea market in New York. The wooden chairs are from Copenhagen and the floor lamp is midcentury modern stainless-steel. **opposite bottom** In the studio's viewing room, Eckart's art elucidates its maker's intent: "My interest is in the depiction and expression of transcendentalist and spiritual themes since the beginning of the Renaissance." Works from left: *Layered Zootrope Painting,* 2006; *Endless Line Painting—CNC Type,* 1999, a triptych from the couple's personal collection; *Square Monochrome Painting,* 1988; and *Regular Painting,* circa 2000. **left** The hallway that connects both warehouse structures forms a T-shaped footprint, which Eckart turned into his CD library. **below** In the dining room, Eckart's tour-de-force *3 Unit Superimposed Circuit Painting,* 2006, engages with the indigo-hued vitrine that was designed as a monolith to divide the living room from the kitchen. A midcentury stainless-steel-and-glass dining table is paired with Eames office chairs.

BONNIE PURVIS AND RALPH EDWARD PURVIS, JR.

Decorator Michelle Nussbaumer has just put down her ever-bleating cell phone. She yells out to no one in particular, "She's sending over a chandelier—and a bear!" The "she" is her dear client, who dwells here amid fine French antiques and a stuffed dik-dik or two. The crystal chandelier and the taxidermy bear? Well, that's just another delivery on just another day from the client's vast storage space. Nussbaumer, you see, has gotten used to this—and, in the process, has found a kindred spirit.

Nussbaumer met her client (of good Swedish stock, and a fanatic collector of eighteenth-century French furniture) just after the client and her family (a strapping, sportsman husband and two strapping, sportsman sons) had sold their big manse. This time they wanted a twist: a "kind of 'loft' thing," said the client to Nussbaumer. A hunt ensued. The trophy? A ninth-floor space in an immense, 1910 downtown building that was once a Sears, Roebuck and Company catalog merchandise center. One problem: One loft wasn't enough to accommodate the family's favorite things—things that include a Louis XVI console, myriad deer mounts, a huge plaster Byzantine Madonna and a stuffed alligator, positioned in full swim, mouth agape. "I said to the client," reports Nussbaumer, "'Let's just go downstairs to the front desk and see if we can get the loft next door'—and we did."

Once a doorway was punched between the two, all decorating hell broke loose. More animals were trucked in. More antiques, too. Nussbaumer laughs that the wide-eyed building staff must've thought, "They're moving a whole château up there!" In came settees, urns, bergères, paintings, Oushak rugs, and blue-and-white porcelains. ("I found the one person who has more stuff than I do," says Nussbaumer.) Decorator and client relished working together, sharing decorating passions and sensibilities, including the European one of loving one's furnishings and living with them and *on* them. Says Nussbaumer: "The dog is on the sofa, the cat is running around, and the sons come in and drop their bows and arrows everywhere." Certainly, nothing is too precious here, in this purely industrial space that has now had a French manor house *and* a big-game lodge deftly inserted into it by Nussbaumer, herself a world traveler and collector, known to send e-mails—after weeks of being incommunicado—that read "In Switzerland. With the children."

The contrasts within this ethereal, elegant space are thrilling: pipes and concrete versus silk and cane, antique furniture playing off the former warehouse's gorgeously nicked and scratched floors. This reverie is fleeting. Nussbaumer's cell phone tweets again. "It's the bear!" she says out loud, to no one in particular. "It's here."

opposite An eighteenth-century Italian pricket is adapted as a lamp, with a shade of Fortuny fabric. A nineteenth-century French chair poses in front of a door that once hung in a château. The silvered mirror is eighteenth-century French; the blue-and-white porcelain is from the Chiang dynasty. Decorator Michelle Nussbaumer whimsically likens the loft's concrete support columns to "modern versions of the columns at Luxor Temple" in Egypt.

opposite An eighteenth-century French settee wears creamy, ivory leather. Nussbaumer devised the hanging burlap "walls" to divide the open loft— an example of her deft pairing of the magnificent with the mundane. *above* Industrial meets ethereal in this corner of the main space. The Venetian mirror is one of a pair; it hangs over a period Louis XVI daybed piled with pillows made from Aubussons and silks. The Chinese trunk at center is covered in pigskin. At left is a gathering of Italian and Moorish pottery. *right* A sterling-silver chandelier awaits its big moment. Until then, it rests in a seventeenth-century Indian baby bed made of bronze. *following page left* In the second bedroom, a mounted alligator swims over a trio of nature photographs taken by the husband and an assortment of hunting ephemera that includes bows, felt hats, a gun, and a feathered turkey carcass. *following page right* A Fortuny lamp stands beside a Louis XV sofa, also in Fortuny. Over the sofa hangs one of a pair of fanci-ful Venetian mirrors, its twin, hung across the loft, reflected in it. Nussbaumer arrived at the pale-blue wall color used throughout the loft by thinking of "all those great château colors" and, of course, at nine stories up, "living in the sky."

opposite At one end of the "hunting lodge" side of the loft, a dik-dik guards a 1980s work by artist Dan Rizzie. The nineteenth-century French chair—its upholstery beautifully tattered—holds a pillow made from modern ikat fabric designed by Nussbaumer. The loft's industrial leanings are quite evident in the roll-up metal door left in situ. *above left* Oh, deer. Just a few of the trophies brought back by the Purvis men, mounted over a set of antique bird prints that belonged to Purvis's grandfather. Folded at the end of the bed is nineteenth-century African Kuba cloth. *above right* A Byzantine Madonna and child made of plaster watch over the master bedroom. Nineteenth-century garden urns perch on nineteenth-century pedestals. The antique rug was woven in Tabriz. *right* One of two bedroom spaces in the loft, this one is set with an iron canopy bed that's been refreshingly relieved of all its draperies; the throw is made of nineteenth-century saris. Over the headboard hangs an antique barometer ringed with shell plates. Its hands went missing in the move to the loft.

opposite top This chartreuse lair houses an octagonal seventeenth-century Italian library table, pulled up to a red-velvet Knole-style sofa. On the table is a James Surls maquette. The large mixed-media work above the sofa is by the San Francisco artist J. W. King. *opposite bottom far left* On a guest-bedroom wall is a series of paintings by the Philadelphia portrait artist Rebecca Westcott. They hang above a large wall piece by the New York artist Taylor McKimens. A seventeenth-century Italian walnut cassapanca (trunk with a seat atop it) rests beneath a Mexican Olinalá trunk. *opposite left* In the master bedroom, the Chinese headboard was originally part of a much larger religious altar. The mid–nineteenth-century Chinese lanterns have rosewood stands. Artwork, from left: lithograph by Cy Twombly; stitchery landscape by the San Francisco artist Tony Cox; a portrait of Mickey Mouse by Joyce Pensato, from Texas Gallery. *above* In the dining room are Anglo-Indian dining chairs and a table. The cobalt-blue resin sculpture on the dining-room table is by Roxy Paine. The *Lucky L* painting is by the San Francisco artist Barry McGee, with "floaters" by Chris Johanson hanging in the foreground. The Bakelite-and-velvet frieze at the edge of the ceiling is from a now-demolished Warner Bros. movie theater in Hollywood and was picked up at the Rose Bowl Flea Market in Pasadena. *right* A pair of wrought-iron-and-gilt Italian candelabras flanks a Spanish colonial santo bust.

opposite In this living-room detail is a late–nineteenth-century carved Rajasthan guard and a bronze Chinese bat sensor from Blackman Cruz, Los Angeles. The Joe Mancuso wall sculpture is made of wood. Taxidermy bobcats, are beside Hispano-Moresque luster vases with an antique Olinalá lacquerware charger from Mexico. **above left** In this alcove bath, walls painted fire-engine red play against gunmetal-finish tile. A dragon-shaped Balinese faucet is above an antique Indian vanity. The bold 1950s Mexican mirror ensconced in iron scrollwork is by Jose Guadalupe Sanchez. **above** In the dining room, an eighteenth-century silk-and-gold-thread tapestry from the estate of Rudolph Valentino is the backdrop for a Mexican wrought-iron altar-candle stand. Atop it is a sculpture by Donald Lipski. Beneath it, a seventeenth-century cassone. **left** In the living room, the goatskin-covered panels of the above-window frieze were fabricated by the late Lynn Ford, architect O'Neil Ford's brother. It once lined the walls of a Jean-Michel Frank–inspired library. The series of watercolors hanging in the frieze is by the artist Eric Pearce. The carved bas-relief over the fireplace is by Aaron Spangler. The Pedro Friedeberg coffee table is in the form of a gilded serpent with a Spanish colonial santo head. The wrought-iron fireplace screen by Hunt Diederich depicts hounds on a kill.

LISA POPE AND GREG WESTERMAN

Soon after launching her eponymous design firm, Lisa Pope Westerman began drafting plans for a speculative house set on a lush, tree-rich site, to be cleverly cantilevered over a fault—yes, an earthquake fault. Then she learned she was expecting twins. As she visited the quaint cul-de-sac to work on the project, she had a revelation: Could there be a more perfect place for her own family?

"The big focus of this house was how it was going to transition between adults and children," she says. "I needed to keep the kind of contemporary sophistication that's appropriate for an urban-ite, but also the functionality you need for children." With a strong restaurant-design background garnered during her tenure at designer David Rockwell's New York City firm, Pope Westerman (who holds a master's degree in architecture) prefers to work in volumes and then think about what the experience will be like in that given space. Case in point: Enter the foyer with its lower ceiling, and you are led to the big wow, the higher-ceilinged living area. "It's important to me to create a variety of experiences," she says. "What I did was create sub-rooms."

In Pope Westerman–speak, sub-rooms are flexible spaces that adapt to different needs dur-ing different times of your life. For example, step up and out of the living area and into a durable, Marmoleum-floored space that doubles as an art studio where kids can paint and an office where adults can log in serious computer time. Wait a decade, and the room will be transformed into a li-brary. Pope Westerman says her husband was the client in this scenario. "He grounded the space, to a degree," she says, "whereas I could live in a test-case home that's really out there and experimental."

For a slice of the unexpected, turn a corner, and you'll find one of the residual spaces that Pope Westerman has elevated to jewel-like status: A Dan Flavin–inspired installation casts light upon a reading nook in the master bedroom, while another installation in the entry glows from within—a nod to James Turrell. The billboard-like art installation on the home's facade? That's a photographic reflection of the surrounding landscape that, along with giant numerals announcing the street address, wraps around the corner of the house.

No matter how much fun Pope Westerman had designing her house, she still had to deal with that big, scary earthquake fault. She built the structure forty-two inches above the ground upon a structural steel framing system with a concrete pier foundation to shore it, so that the house adjusts to shifts in the earth. (By cantilevering the house over the fault, she also extended the square footage.) "It's my way of playing with the fault line," she says. "I may not be allowed to be on you, but I'm hovering right over you."

opposite A modern vignette in the living room: In the window is a trio of decorative vases collected by the homeowners.

50

opposite above left Beneath a trio of shell chandeliers are a vintage Danish modern dining table and chairs. A curtain partitions the dining and media rooms. **opposite above right** On the home's facade is a custom billboard of the address by Chris Promecene. **opposite bottom** The open kitchen—outfitted with IKEA's red-lacquered cabinets, customized to fit, and custom-marble countertops—flows into the dining room and breakfast area. Hanging on the walls are an Eames splint and a trio of Fornasetti plates. The porcelain-glazed floor tiles are of Spanish slab blanco. **above** In the living room is Philippe Starck's Mademoiselle chair for Kartell. The custom Carrara marble–topped, steel-framed desk is by Alberto Bonomi. The sofa is by Jonathan Adler. The antique Chinese cabinet was lacquered jade green, then coated in gold polyurethane by Pope Westerman herself. **right** The master-bedroom reading area has a Dan Flavin–inspired light installation, created by Pope Westerman from fluorescent lights. The lounge armchair is vintage Eames Aluminum Group. **following pages** The living room has a paneled wall of custom rift-cut oak. A pair of vintage Eames Aluminum Group lounge chairs. The vintage modern cocktail table was inherited, and the caned Mies van der Rohe–like side chair was a Goodwill find.

HIRAM BUTLER

Some men dream of being ensconced in a palazzo above the canals of Venice or in a remote castle on the Scottish moors. But gallery owner Hiram Butler dreams of having a closet. Unpretentious and forthright, this partner in the acclaimed Devin Borden Hiram Butler Gallery is living in a circa-1880 German immigrant worker's house that he's beautifully restored during the past fifteen years, a stone's throw from his gallery. "My dream is to one day have a closet," the irreverent Butler says. "I am going to add it to the end of the bedroom. I want one of those walk-in closets . . . with a wall for your Judith Leiber bags."

While he possesses not one glittering Leiber clutch, the dealer who early in his career honed his taste working at the Museum of Modern Art now avidly collects prints as well as dynamic artwork. "I tend to own work on paper . . . I think in large part because it is also portable," says Butler, whose collection includes prints by Jasper Johns, Cy Twombly, Andy Warhol and Robert Rauschenberg.

The humble house Butler inhabits, with its white-painted walls, high ceilings, and wide-plank cypress hardwoods, was built before 1880. "It had sat vacant for some time," he says. "Chain-link fencing was stored inside, and it had sunken badly." He undertook a long list of structural repairs to restore the six-room, 950-square-foot structure. In keeping with its integrity, he did not reconfigure the rooms. After much contemplation, however, he removed the wainscoting from everywhere but the front hall, as it impeded his ability to hang art. That's when he discovered there was no standard insulation in the walls. Instead, he found four to five feet of stored pecans buried between the studs by squirrels that had once taken up residence there. He installed not only insulation but also central air-conditioning and a new tin roof. Needless to say, the standard outhouse was eliminated, and indoor plumbing for the property's first bathroom was installed.

From sunrise to sunset, the interior of the home is bathed with light—a stunning effect, but a hazard for anyone who collects serious works on paper. Serendipitously, on a foray to Richard Meier's new art center in Des Moines, Butler found the solution: white packing Styrofoam, sized and cut to fit each window. The effect beautifully filters the streams of light.

Seamlessly bridging his work and home life, Butler's house is situated across the garden from his Mies van der Rohe–inspired gallery. An allée of oleander trees creates a fragrant archway between the structures. At noon, Butler and staff close up shop to break for lunch served at the Butler residence. An avid Southern cook, Butler turns these meals into meetings, and you never know who might drop in.

opposite In the dining room, the Arts and Crafts fruitwood cabinet is filled with Egyptian, Roman, and South Asian antiquities. The oldest dates to 3000 B.C. The photograph by Sherrie Levine is from *The Barcham Greene Portfolio* series, after Walker Evans's piece entitled *Sharecropper's Wife*.

preceding pages In Hiram Butler's bedroom hangs a large woodcut, *Big 5,* by Jonathan Borofsky. Also pictured are a Shaker-style bed with a quilt, a Luxo lamp, and *Shadow Chair* by Robert Wilson. On the wall, in an obscured view, is a suite of ten Agnes Martin prints. *opposite top* The dining table by sculptor Michael Scranton is flanked by six Stendig bentwood caned chairs. A triptych of Robert Rauschenberg's lithographs entitled *Autobiography* encompasses nearly an entire wall. *opposite bottom right* In the living room, a settee was a junk-store find. The etching is *Face with Watch* by Jasper Johns. In the foreground is a plywood cube by the sculptor Dean Ruck. The hammer sculpture is by Sheila Rosenstein. *opposite bottom far right* Above the claw-and-ball-foot table by Daryl Lauster is a series of etchings, *The Barcham Greene Portfolio,* by Sherrie Levine. The pot is nineteenth-century Texas pottery made by slaves. *above* Hanging on the original painted doors of the living-room entry is a Jasper Johns lithograph, *Ventriloquist*. To the left is Tony Feher's untitled piece made of wrappers from Reese's Peanut Butter Cups and notary seals. Below it is Nestor Topchy's *Night and Day*. *left* In the entry hall, the large-scale color photograph *Roden Crater Painted Desert Arizona,* by James Turrell, hangs above a canary-yellow-painted pine table. The dark-stained wide-plank floors, original to the house, are made of cypress.

GEORGE SELLERS

George Sellers has a secret. And it's right there among gritty little clubs, a cutting-edge art gallery or two and a corner restaurant that serves meatloaf and mashed potatoes. For stirred into this most urban of environments is Sellers's hyper-chic lair. David Hicks gone high. A worldly place that is, quite literally, a stage set for Sellers's colorful life, divided into scenes by silky white curtains and always ready for the next opening night.

Man met loft when Sellers moved his life to Dallas from New York, by way of—in reverse order—Sarasota, Florida; Italy; Singapore; Indonesia; Saudi Arabia; Graham, Oklahoma; White Deer, Texas; and, the start of it all, Dimmit, Texas. ("One letter off of 'dammit,'" Sellers says, "and a little hellhole of a farm town in the panhandle.") The globe-trotting was thanks to Dad's work for Mobil Oil. The life lessons and aesthetic picked up along the way? That's all George. He picked up something else, too: a double degree in ceramic sculpture and art history, exorcising his creative demons designing furniture and lighting and creating powerful figurative sculpture, all of which surround him in his highly personal home.

Sellers swooned upon seeing the fifteen-hundred-square-foot loft because, coming directly from New York, "it was the most 'city' place I could find." It also was a blank canvas, nothing but exposed-truss ceilings, bare walls, and a poured-concrete floor. "It was a box with plumbing—and the rest is whatever I wanted to do." Which meant dividing the loft into transformable zones by hanging silky white curtains from metal tubes and devising an articulated divider wall, made of a pine frame and stretched muslin, to bisect the main space. Sellers got the idea, like so many of his ideas, from another project he'd been working on, this one a ballet set he had designed. Scrims for the stage became scrims for his space.

And a lively space it is. Sexy music moves through it freely. Friends drop by with regularity. Miss Mapp, a wise old cat named for a fictional literary British schemer and social climber, stretches out on her moss-green 1960s lounge chair. But the star of this show is Sellers himself, gliding about the place, quoting *Auntie Mame* with startling precision and rattling off encyclopedic tidbits about everything from tragic figures in history to the 1966 Volvo P1800 coupe he's restoring—you know, "the one the original Saint drove on TV, not the later Saint." He can also tell you the story of every piece in the place, from a rare Knoll butterfly chair to a rusted teapot rescued from a shipwreck. George Sellers loves a good story—and here in this secret space, he's hit his mark.

opposite One of two living areas in the loft: The cement torso sculptures are by George Sellers. The tulip-base table in the center of the room is "not a Saarinen," Sellers says. "I don't even think it aspires to be a Saarinen." The pierced-ceramic hanging lamp hails from a Luby's cafeteria.

opposite The burned chair in the foreground is by Teyah O'Quinn, who designs under the simple label P. It has been sealed with six coats of polyurethane, and the seat is upholstered in black leather. The X-leg table holds a collection of what Sellers jokingly calls "government-issue Murano crap." The stepped table against the wall is a Sellers design in ebonized pine. *above* The bedroom space has a George Sellers–designed bed of zebrawood and hair-on cowhide. He found the collapsible light structure in a roadside shop. Why the Prada suitcase? "You have to carry on a *little* something that's good for the soul," Sellers says. He found the highly polished chrome David Rowland chair at a flea market, not knowing its status as a modern classic. "It's shiny. I go for shiny. Just like a bass." *left* Sellers concocted the mirror using an old frame that held one of his drawings. "I sold the drawing but kept the frame!" The twin chair-stools are from an Art Deco bar at Tulsa's Biltmore Hotel, now destroyed. The sculptural monolith at far right, titled *Fool,* is by the artist Pamela Mahaffey Rossing. The white chair, foreground right, is an ongoing Sellers project. "It *was* mahogany. It's been silver-leafed, gold-leafed, and now painted white. It just doesn't care anymore."

opposite One side of the living area has a vintage Knoll butterfly chair in its rare, original leather sling and a rare matching stool. The credenza is shared by a classical dolphin candlestick by Sellers; a teak Indonesian Garuda, a symbol of protection ("He's a good demon," Sellers says); and a Sellers lamp entitled *Full Moon on Wing,* made of walnut and aluminum leaf, with fused glass by Diana Chase. On the George Sellers coffee table is a terra-cotta *Lotus Pod* sculpture by Pamela Mahaffey Rossing. *above* In the foreground, the open dining area has a Heywood-Wakefield table ringed by 1940s French chairs in their original tufted patent leather, which Sellers would never dream of changing. "They're a little rough," he says. "They've been around town." Overhead is a mad-scientist creation of sockets and bulbs by Sellers. Between the dining and living spaces is a George Sellers sculpture in carved plaster (à la Henry Moore) titled *Seated Male*. The star of the living room is the vintage sofa, stuffed with down, and upholstered in dark-orange mohair. The coffee table with its five male figures supporting a thick glass top is also by Sellers. The bookcases hold global finds and tomes on Mozart, the Bolshoi, Leonardo da Vinci, E. E. Cummings, Flemish art, M. C. Escher, and *Pleasure of Ruins*. *right* A plaster monster by artist Joe Ely.

JAMES McINROE

Decorator James McInroe doesn't settle down for long. He is, by his own admission, ready to move again as soon as the last baseboard dries and the last drapery panel goes up, and he's proven himself a truth-teller so far: five residences in as many years, including moving once within the same building.

And then, the fateful phone call. "It's James. I've moved again. I think you should come see it. I must say, it's pretty posh."

This means it's *extremely* posh. He's not one to brag. In fact, it's one of his notable qualities: a certain shyness and humbleness about the oh-wows heaped upon him. There is likely no one who has walked into a James McInroe interior—especially one of McInroe's own abodes—and not had a strong reaction. Take that for what you will. His client list is peppered with strong-willed, colorful, highly individual characters. (What would Freud have to say about that?) In fact, maybe it's all rooted in color itself: McInroe mixes his strong and a little off. He's been toying with odd greens and Tiffany blues for years, cutting them with shocks of vibrant orange and twisted, fire-engine reds. But here, on the top floor of a 1930s Tudor, he's gone darker, richer, deeper. The living room is saturated in a murky brown-black, the color of morel mushrooms. The adjoining sunroom pulsates in rich acid green, while the kitchen and bath are a storm-cloud gray. And the bedroom? An olive drab zinged up with velvet curtains in burnt Hermès orange. You may need a drink.

Which is precisely what this small apartment seems suited for. You can almost imagine Dorothy Parker and pals lighting up the barbs and cigarettes while ice clinks in their highballs. With its cave-like coziness and era-jumping jumble of party-perfect furniture, it's nighttime all the time in this tiny little Tudor. (This fact is not lost on McInroe, whose whole take on this dark thing is thus: "I think it's okay to do an apartment just for the night. Who's ever home in the daytime?") And like any good party, things change fast here. Pieces come and go. Rooms get flipped. Those Brno chairs you remembered over there got moved over here. That English armoire in the bedroom is likely to work its way into the living room.

Restless, is he? This mod scientist always seems to be churning and turning things—in his mind and otherwise. It's probably that tortured-creative-type thing that infects the best brains. Whatever it is, all you can do is settle into McInroe's white-leather lounge chairs, call up Parker and Freud, pour some Scotch, and see what *they* think.

opposite James McInroe's walk-through sunroom connects the living room to the kitchen. He theorizes that the Art Deco pedestal table is Austrian or German. Flanking it, Donghia's modern-classic Anziano chairs, designed for Villa Aurelia at the American Academy in Rome. Overhead, a 1970s Lucite-and-chrome chandelier.

opposite The living room's 1960s cowhide chair gets cozy with a 1950s folding cigarette table and a classic Cedric Hartman floor lamp. *above* This living room swings, from its 1830 French *Restauration* bronze-and-marble candlesticks on a 1930 Mies van der Rohe glass-and-stainless-steel cocktail table to the 1950s Florence Knoll sofa, over which hang eighteenth-century Italian engravings. The two Ward Bennett leather-upholstered chairs face off with a 1960s lounge chair of questionable pedigree, partly upholstered in hairy cowhide. The Sputnik lamp is from "sometime around the space program," McInroe says, "whenever that was." *below* McInroe's showstopping Biedermeier bed is butted against 1970s cotton-velvet curtains. The armoire, far right, is English, 1950s. The bench is by T. H. Robsjohn-Gibbings. The chair is "French *Restauration*," McInroe says, "from the first quarter of the nineteenth century" and upholstered in silk with a repeating bumblebee motif.

KEN DOWNING AND SAM SALADINO

Diana Vreeland would've loved this place. The late, great fashion editor was always going on about the magic ingredient she believed would add zing to any instance of absolute exquisite taste: paprika. Hers was a hypothetical thought, of course, but anything that would throw off a studied moment was, she said, like "a splash" of the stuff. This house is dusted in D.V.'s paprika. Owners Ken Downing (the senior vice president and fashion director of Neiman Marcus) and Sam Saladino (a superstar sales associate for same, and a stylist of chic model residences) specialize in that particular brand of zing. To wit: Powerful, visceral works by contemporary painters are roused by a no-name canvas that Saladino picked up in Tampa because he "just liked it." Or the living room, where a ceramic zebra cohabits with straight-lined Florence Knoll club chairs and a glittery crystal candelabrum. Even in the master bedroom, the sleek, modernist bed and the mid-century chairs are taken down a notch by a pair of jumbo, curvy brass lamps, scored at a country flea market. So it goes at the Downing-Saladino manse—the high with the low, the exquisite with the witty.

The house was lucky to have found them. The partners discovered the modernist brick rambler ten years ago, when loft living had run its course. "The bones were good," says Downing of the house, which was built between 1954 and 1956, "but everything was pink—walls, carpet, everything. It looked like Alexandra de Markoff foundation in here." Up went calm, cool white. Down went brick floors the color of Cor-Ten steel after it has developed its wonderful, dark coating. (Downing, a compulsive straightener, likes the floors for a different reason: "You can grid furniture out and know *exactly* where you are!") Outside, iron grilles were pulled off the windows and, to tap into the structure's floating, Japanese-teahouse quality, a striking palette of sage green and spicy orange was slicked on the trim and doors. The result? A swank place more '60s in vernacular than its '50s roots. Downing and Saladino retained the house's unique details, too, such as the gigantic living-room fireplace, with its dramatic marble hood and, of course, the expansive walls of glass onto the lush, garden-like front lawn. "You know," says Saladino, laughing, "we *love* our vistas," making reference to his and Downing's passion for all things visual, not only for spectacular views but for urbane clothes and inspired furniture, for flea-market art and Baroque splendor, for antique Iranian rugs and Elsie de Wolfe. Because of it, the house indeed resonates with dashes of Vreeland's favorite spice.

opposite The room that Sam Saladino calls "our little cabinet of curiosities" is propped with a glamorous mishmash that includes a Lucite chair found at an antiques mall, an African mask won on eBay, and a vintage lamp of rather Roman leanings. The "Dirk" painting is by Ludwig Schwarz.

opposite A zebra with a view—of the living room's original marble-and-brick fireplace. *above* The library corner of the capacious living room. The Brutalist table lamp at far left is a Paul Evans design; the swank bench is attributed to Greek designer Nicos Zographos. The library table was from a Los Angeles auction. The art is a mix of works by Jeff Elrod, Josephine Mahaffey, Victor Vasarely, and George Sharp. *below* In a living room made just for lounging, reinterpreted Florence Knoll club chairs and a vintage sofa gather around an antique Persian rug. The line painting, background right, is by Susie Rosmarin. A Carlo Scarpa chandelier dangles over a vintage Mies van der Rohe daybed.

opposite The entry hall features a bench in the manner of T. H. Robsjohn-Gibbings, a brass table found at a consignment shop, and a pair of vintage lamps. **above** What would be a breakfast nook anywhere else is, instead, a moment of artful repose. An Alexander Calder leans against the wall. **below** The dining room features a powerful painting by Ludwig Schwarz and a Saarinen marble-topped table. The light fixture is vintage, from the Los Angeles Police Department. The cane-back chairs were also found in Los Angeles and were "spray-painted gold," Downing says, "and upholstered in pink taffeta—like bad bridesmaids' gowns."

AARON RAMBO

Stylist-turned-decorator Aaron Rambo is on a perpetual quest for authenticity. As co-owner of a vintage and antiques shop named Found, his only mandate is that each piece in his store, regardless of its provenance, must have undeniable authenticity. "I like juxtaposition," he says. "The only rule: I don't like fake stuff. I divide my world into thirds—a third that's classic eighteenth- and nineteenth-century (serious Louis XVI and drippy chandeliers) and a third midcentury . . . The other third is industrial pieces, because not a lot of people are doing that."

True to form, at home Rambo is ensconced on the second floor of a nineteenth-century loft, an old brick building where for decades artists have found shelter and perhaps even inspiration. "You know the cup holders they used to have for your car that slid into the window before cup holders [were] built into your car? They manufactured those here, in this building," he says. "It was also a furniture company—Bienville Furniture Company." Here, inside his marvelously merchandised home with its crumbling mortar, singed rafters overhead (the third floor burned down years ago), and few dividers partitioning one area from another (save for the bath and a closet topped by a bed), Rambo's personal space resembles his work environs. Or is it vice versa? Lines blur, and ideas converge brilliantly.

Several years ago, Rambo's "nothing but real" credo made him itch to move from his "fake loft," despite the luxury of its top-of-the-line appliances and modern conveniences. "I'm downgrading, sort of," he says. "But if you're going to be in a loft, get a real one—preferably a nineteenth-century one." It's here that the man on a perpetual hunt for the overlooked and the forgotten lives, amid straitlaced sofas that blend seamlessly with industrial pieces: a mechanic's stool beside a tangle of orange electrical cords; disparate drawings, some adhered to the wall with nothing more than blue painter's tape; a giant, rusty ball of barbed wire paired with a collection of all things white, some precious and others merely pretty; and a vintage vegetable display rack topped with an old, oiled, hollow door that serves as a kitchen island.

Rambo gathers his treasures from forays to small towns, estate auctions, and long walks through dicey parts of town. He also scours eBay, which has turned up such wonders as a hand-colored nineteenth-century French anatomical work and a zebra-skin rug. What's his secret? While you or I might overlook a brutalist light fixture made of jagged metal or bypass an old metal salesman's trunk, Rambo recognizes them as, respectively, the centerpiece of his living area and the missing step on a flight of stairs—jewels among the detritus that awaits him on each scavenger's stalk.

opposite In Aaron Rambo's home office, a nineteenth-century elmwood farm table serves as a desk. Eighteenth-century painted Swedish stool. Zebra skin found on eBay. The French scientific chalkboard depicts cross-sections of a cat and a rabbit.

opposite In the living area, situated in a center of the loft space, is a bentwood Ply Craft chair, circa 1965. A nineteenthth-century French garden table serves as the cocktail table. A brutalist brass lighting fixture hangs overhead. *above left* Vintage flat-file art-storage bureau. Faux-grained door is nineteenth-century French, from Argentina. French postal bag in custom acrylic box. The four hanging metal objects are hat molds. *above right* On the table, a ball of rusted barbed wire, found at an antiques fair and a collection of all things white. Vintage Louis XVI–style chair is juxtaposed with a pair of mid-century chrome floor lamps. *left* A vintage '70s mirror hangs above an Ebony-painted chest of drawers. *following page right* In the kitchen is an ebony framed mirror in lieu of a kitchen window, that reflects the light streaming in opposite. Custom light fixture created with an industrial wire basket. *following page left* In the foreground of the kitchen is a carved stone architectural fragment set on a leg-less table. The kitchen island is a perforated-steel vegetable display table that started life in an Illinois grocery store, and is now topped with a simple, oiled hollow-core door. It holds a collection of white china and vintage ironstone plates. By the wall is a wooden fruit-picking ladder. Pots and pans hang from

DAVID LACKEY

Imagine the wicked temptation of working in the business of selling objects that you yourself collect. Each day you might be forced to make taxing decisions. Do I part with this rare English Regency armorial platter or keep it for myself? Shall I sell this vintage Louis Vuitton trunk or earmark it for my own collection? (Ultimately you decide the platter goes; the trunk, which just happens to be monogrammed with your own initials, stays home.) Such is the tortured fate of antiques collector, dealer, and appraiser David Lackey, a renowned china authority who has channeled his passion for pottery into a career. Lackey is perhaps best known for his work on the PBS cult hit *Antiques Roadshow*, which commissioned him as an appraiser thirteen years ago. He's also the founder of edish.com, an Internet-based china-and-crystal company that sleuths out previously owned and discontinued patterns. As he unearths long-forgotten treasures for his clients, he quells his own peculiar penchant for objects so wacky that he delights in the very thought of them.

Nearly every corner of the eccentric town house he shares with partner Russell Prince is chockablock with high charm and wildly disparate treasures, including a rare pattern of precious English Spode Imari colored porcelain; crested and armorial British Regency ceramics; three early nineteenth-century Anglo-Indian ebony side chairs (from an original set of six, the others reside in a museum); English Derby entomological porcelain dessert plates, circa 1815, bought at auction in London; a George Nakashima table commissioned by Warhol in 1957, acquired at Warhol's Sotheby's auction; Louisiana tourist art; faux-painted furniture; and eighteenth- and nineteenth-century English and European boxes. And there are vernacular photographs—snapshots from the 1930s, '40s, and '50s depicting shoppers on the street, as well as blue-toned candids clicked a century ago—and souvenir sterling-silver spoons with alligator handles. Icing the Yves Klein–blue and mossy-green walls like plaster moldings are more than one hundred Spode and Coalport shell-shaped serving dishes, thirteen white parian busts, and eighteenth-century framed portraits and wildlife drawings.

Despite his educated and discriminating eye, Lackey never shuns the humble for the haute. His own house exemplifies his appreciation of quirky furnishings with a pedigree, as well as his affinity for objets that he calls "wonderfully awful." In the main house's powder room, for example, crustaceans and tortoises repose in the bath; the guest cottage shelters his wicked bluebonnet painting collection—a quirky assemblage that might make the most uptight antiquarian shudder. Refreshingly, not the madcap Mr. Lackey.

opposite The early nineteenth-century marble-topped French Empire pier table is laden with David Lackey's collection of bulbous vases of varying values. The bust beneath is a nineteenth-century marble replica. Ebony side chairs are early nineteenth-century Anglo-Indian, with seats covered in Fortuny. Oil painting, circa 1945, is by New Orleans artist Paul Ninas.

preceding page left The library is a repository of books and collections, such as carpet balls perched on candlesticks and glorious armorial china. Tufted Edwardian leather chairs and Roseville pottery lamp with mica shade. The coffee table is George Nakashima, commissioned by Andy Warhol in 1957 and bought by Lackey at Sotheby's Warhol auction. *preceding page right* The French Gothic Revival walnut bed is dressed in a flax-colored linen spread. Charcoal drawings, academic studies by nineteenth-century Italian artist Giuseppe Guzzardi, frame the bed. A collection of reliquaries hangs behind a pair of silver-plated neoclassical column lamps. Nightstands are early nineteenth-century British pot cupboards. The chair is painted English Regency, circa 1820s. *opposite* In the living room, a channel-back wing chair, one of a pair that flanks a vintage Louis Vuitton monogrammed trunk, coincidentally with Lackey's own monogram. Armorial china and eighteenth-century framed portraits and drawings of wildlife dot the Yves Klein–blue wall. *above* In the master bath, a faux-marble cabinet resembling a capital column is created as a man's dressing table laden with tortoises, Japanese reticulated copper crawfish and a majolica crab, some of which also rest in jest in the bathtub. Portrait of Lackey by artist Patrick Palmer.

ROB DAILEY and TODD FISCUS

Rob Dailey is positively swooning. "We have," says the decorator and furniture designer, taking a deep breath, "this mad love affair with San Miguel." And how. Dailey can offer no better proof than the house he shares with partner Todd Fiscus, an event-planning master of chic society weddings and over-the-top charity events, all with a modern bent. Which may explain the pair's love of the historic, the charming, and the sit-a-spell: Their home, channeling the essence of San Miguel de Allende, the Mexican mountain town rooted in 1542, certainly must be a fast-acting antidote for two harried, hurried lives.

But enough with the armchair psychology. This mad-for-Mexico affair has reached its zenith with this house, built in the mid-1990s in a hilly neighborhood. But this was no love at first sight: The house had been styled as an ersatz Mediterranean, all pink and tiled and gloppy. Inside, not much better. "Carpet, hardwoods, concrete, linoleum," Dailey says. "It looked like the flooring department of a home-improvement store." But the house's generous L-shaped plan, tree-filled lot and gracious outdoor spaces wooed the two. Move over, Club Med; hello San Miguel. "We pretty much scraped the house out," says Dailey. Up went a plasterlike coating to add depth to the ho-hum walls, down went limestone floors from—where else—Mexico. Moroccan windows were popped in here and there. A burbling fountain was centered in the gravel courtyard out back. Carved wooden doors were hung in all the right places.

It wasn't until Dailey and Fiscus started mixing and mingling the furnishings that the house started to sing—but not a slavish tune. The couple's trademark wit comes through loud and clear in the elegantly crazy juxtapositions, the oddly fabulous contrasts. In the living room, a damask-covered French settee pulls up to a sleek Lucite box of a coffee table. A tall, golden twig of a floor lamp looks suspiciously like a Diego Giacometti had taken a turn through Twin Peaks. Even in the master bedroom, a pristine white Barcelona chair nudges up to a Chinese cabinet whose paint is falling off by the minute and where the sumptuous bed gains a little levity from the modernist-Baroque headboard (a Dailey design) in persimmon velvet with zippy nailhead trim. Modern art almost everywhere adds a delicious tension to the curvy, comfy furnishings. All over this highly refined hacienda, it's the funny with the fine, the contemporary with the cozy. Where the house truly excels? When friends spill onto the arched and columned loggia to settle around the outdoor fireplace for a long night in. Cocktails and ribald stories, guaranteed.

opposite The cozy master bedroom has a custom headboard by Rob Dailey, upholstered in linen velvet and outlined with chromed nail heads. Dailey also designed the pair of Lucite side tables, the left one holding an antique ballot box. The lantern overhead is from San Miguel de Allende. Dailey had an old Indian room divider made into the shutters that cover the windows.

opposite Custom doors of antique longleaf pine reveal the book-lined hallway that leads to the master bedroom. In the bedroom are a Barcelona chair and an antique Chinese chest with a collection of bright-turquoise Chinese-export mud figures. ***above*** The grand loggia has an outdoor fireplace. The luxe tables and chairs are teak, by Sutherland. An antique Moroccan bed is piled with pillows. ***right*** The long dining space holds a sideboard by an Indian artist who covered it in bits and pieces of mirror. Above it hangs a manipulated digital photograph by Ted Kincaid. ***following pages*** The living room is one big culture clash. The sofa is a Rob Dailey design, upholstered in Belgian linen. Dailey also designed the round pillow on the sofa, made with an antique textile, and the Lucite cocktail table. The pair of antique French bergères is wittily upholstered like teddy bears. At right is a monumental work by Nicolas Alquin, executed in ink and black beeswax on glass-fiber paper. Over the French mantel hangs a mid-eighteenth-century Venetian mirror that Dailey found in a back room at Ann Koerner Antiques in New Orleans, a favorite shop. "All good things happen in the back room," Dailey says.

LESTER MARKS

Lester Marks is utterly consumed with a passion for his next art acquisition. His mind, even at rest, races with ideas and negotiations designed to win the latest object of his obsession, which he pursues like a man in love. As a result, his home bursts with one of the most acclaimed and diverse art collections in America: a vast repository of postwar and contemporary works acquired in rapid succession, more than 400 pieces in all, ranging from emerging artists to blue-chip masters, including Robert Rauschenberg, Anselm Kiefer, Andy Warhol, Cy Twombly, Jean-Michel Basquiat, Dan Flavin, and Donald Judd. Small wonder that his passion landed him a place in 2004 on *ARTnews'* lauded list of "The World's Top 200 Collectors."

"I am possessed to the point that when I have a new piece of art arrive in the shipping crate, it may sit for a few days before I have time to open it because I am too busy trying to make a deal on my next piece of art," Marks says. "It's a hunt for the next best piece of art. And the best piece of art . . . is the one I haven't yet bought." Unlike the Lauders, Rockefellers, and movie moguls ranked alongside him in *ARTnews'* annual list, Marks really lives—and lives it up—with his collection. You'll find blue-chip works next to brash newcomers' pieces, all given equal weight, adoration, and praise by the democratic art enthusiast. In his spare time, Marks crafts poetry about how each piece has inspired him. Often he displays these musings behind Plexiglas next to the work itself.

He admits a personal attraction toward sculpture and tends to collect postmodern art with a heavy conceptual slant. "I try and find artists whose work is thoughtful, intelligent, provocative, mysterious—work that doesn't give itself away in a single glance but requires both your heart and your mind," he says. "I have continued to fill every nook and cranny with art, and when I run out of nooks and crannies, I find more ways to build nooks and crannies." The repository for his collection is a 6,000-square-foot contemporary home that includes a quirky, subterranean playpen that one enters from the dining room through a glass door. Inside are floors of white shag, walls of white vinyl, and a Tony Oursler video installation: an eyeball that blinks incessantly.

With Flavin's works serving as his latest obsession, there's no sign of Marks's frenzied buying spree coming to a halt. Friends say he should publish a collection of his writings about art. According to one: "Contemporary art definitely gets enriched by some sort of information—not what this piece means to the artist but about the concept, the current event that was going on at the time." As for the collection's ultimate destiny, Marks says, "I really don't know where it's going. It's a good question, though."

opposite In the dining room, Mario Bellini for Cassina walnut La Rotonda dining table and leather break chairs. Gordon Terry's acrylic-on-acrylic panel, *Black Holes, Bohemians, Colonials, and Boudoirs*, is from New Gallery/Thom Andriola. A Droog chandelier hangs above the dining-room table. Artist McKay Otto's mixed media on canvas, *2087*, is from Barbara Davis Gallery.

opposite In the atrium, the conceptual piece, *Hazeltop Circle*, is by Richard Long, the leading British disciple of Earth Art. On the other side of the atrium is *Sulpicia*, a work from Anselm Kiefer's "Women of Antiquity" series, which tops a painted plaster wedding gown with a 300-pound book with lead pages. Both are from James Cohan Gallery. **above** In the foyer, a pair of sculptures by Joseph Havel is comprised of tiny shirt labels, from Devin Borden Hiram Butler Gallery. Artist Cheryl Kelley's oil on canvas, *Map 8*, is from New Gallery/Thom Andriola. Yigal Ozeri's oil painting on wood, *Royal Dress*, is from Mike Weiss Gallery. **below** In the master bedroom hangs a painted door by Radcliffe Bailey from David Beitzel Gallery. Suspended above the bedside table is Donald Lipski's Untitled, from Barbara Davis Gallery. Above the bed hangs a Kiki Smith drawing of an owl on seven layers of Nepalese tissue paper, from PaceWildenstein.

opposite top left Looking down the stairwell at Louise Bourgeois' fabric sculpture *Regression* in a glass case. Beneath is Tara Conley's *Orb*, from Mike Weiss Gallery. To the right, Larry Bell's mixed media on canvas, *Post 9/11 Tableaux*, from New Gallery/Thom Andriola. At the edge of each step is an installation by Jessica Halonen, who mapped out the diabetes warnings using painted sugar cubes. **opposite top right** In the stairwell is Elena Lopez-Poirot's *Twelve Memories, A Post 9/11 Vision of Remembrances,* from Anya Tish Gallery. **opposite bottom left** On the landing is Mel Ziegler's *Untitled #1*, an antique display cabinet filled with straw, from Michael Klein Gallery. Above it, French tulips by Lisa Ludwig, from Moody Gallery. **opposite bottom right** Works from top: William Betts' digitized acrylic-on-Plexiglas painting, from Poissant Gallery; Cy Twombly's *Roma*, a 1957 oil on canvas; a piece from an unknown French artist; and *Green Piece,* a mixed-media assemblage by Sofi Zezmer, from Mike Weiss Gallery. **above** In the living room, a large-scale piece by German neo-Expressionist Anselm Kiefer called *Merkaba* — the Hebrew word for "Divine Chariot," represented here as an aircraft carrier scattered with lost souls, from Gagosian Gallery. In the foreground is another Anselm Kiefer piece, *Fur Dr. Robert Fludd*, from James Cohan Gallery. **right** Joseph Cornell's *Suzy's Room,* circa 1954, is accompanied by a musing by Lester Marks.

de l'Etoile

ERIC PROKESH

Open the front door to Eric Prokesh's unassuming brick residence—once a neglected rental building that he painstakingly renovated—and you're immediately hit with bursts of bright color. An entry stairwell is papered in a vibrant grass green, and from there you can see the living room, which explodes with turquoise-painted walls, and windows hung with iridescent crimson taffeta. In the living area, there are two eighteenth-century bergères upholstered in luscious Concord-grape silk and a painted Directoire canapé. A fine Swedish nineteenth-century Beidermeier chest anchors a wall. Prokesh added a simply carved mantle in aubergine marble and topped it with an exceptional Charles X gilt clock from France.

"I wanted the colors to be clear, honest, and confident," Prokesh says of his brazen use of pop color in his duplex. "Rather than buy mediocre period paintings—the good stuff is virtually inaccessible—I decided to let the walls add color." The effect is startling and manages to be both contemporary and classic. Is there a method to his madness for all this color? Using hues not normally associated with period furniture forces you to see things with a fresh eye. Brilliant tones also help bring out the furniture's fine qualities, because the sinuous curve of a chair leg or the sheen of eighteenth-century wood is thrown into much higher relief than if the piece is placed against a plain white wall. Besides, color keeps things fun. "I didn't want things to get too serious in here by putting eighteenth-century sconces with the clock and the gilded mirror," Prokesh says. "It's too slavishly period."

Each room in the house is a testament to contrast. The dining room is strong amber with iridescent taffeta curtains that cast a gray or lilac tone, like the breast of a pigeon. "I think decorating with strong color should be controlled as tightly as with a neutral palette," he says. "That's what makes it contemporary." On an intellectual level, these colors might seem brazen, but to the eye they're actually not jarring, but pleasing. The tones are based on classic decorating schemes from the Directoire period, where emerald green was routinely combined with gold, or bright yellow with amethyst. But here's where Prokesh veers again: Instead of cluttering surfaces with random decorative bibelots, he has pared his accessories down to just a very few fine groups. Scattered throughout the apartment are a Tanagra figurine, Sung dynasty bowls, and a collection of Roman glass. "I'm at a point," he says, "where I don't want any more on a table than the eye can bear."

opposite Anchoring the guest room is a fine Austrian cherry Biedermeier daybed, lavishly dressed in cerise-and-oyster striped silk. Designer Eric Prokesh retained the old persimmon-colored velvet upholstery on the eighteenth-century white-painted bergère.

opposite The chartreuse dining room opens to an aqua living room with two eighteenth-century bergères, one upholstered in Concord-grape-and-silver silk damask. **above** Prokesh's office, formerly a sun porch, is spare with creamy travertine floors, a seventeenth-century Henry IV walnut desk and eighteenth-century Louis XVI chairs. **below** Iridescence—found in upholstery, curtains, and even tile—is a theme throughout the house. A portiere in celadon taffeta embroidered with overscaled pomegranate paisley separates the guest room, foreground, from Prokesh's office.

opposite The dining room has an eighteenth-century gilt mirror and marble-topped Directoire console. The dining-room table is draped in fern-and-fawn cotton damask and set with Prokesh's collection of Old Paris porcelain and eighteenth-century English silver. *above* Because the walls, the ceiling, and even the window frames are painted the same cerulean blue, the bedroom seems to float in an ethereal cloud. *right* A Swedish Biedermeier chest is topped with Prokesh's collection of ancient glass, Chinese porcelain, and a rare Tanagra figurine that embodies Prokesh's obsession for fine things. He says: "The day I bought the Tanagra at auction while in college, my power was cut off because I couldn't afford to pay the light bill."

RICHARD HOLLEY

They say that once you discover your passion—something you can toil at blissfully from nine to five, and then some—you'll never work a day in your life. Decorator Richard Holley happily considers work and play interchangeable. Holley, whose interiors have been lauded in *Architectural Digest* and *House Beautiful*, spends his free time poring over an exhaustive home library dedicated to decorating, art, and design—not to mention classic novels, biographies, and mysteries—in search of inspiration. And when that inspiration hits, whether it's 3 p.m. or 3 a.m., Holley wanders no further from his circa-1920 Craftsman-style duplex than across his garden, to a 1950s-era cinderblock "bunker," as he fondly refers to his office complex next door, to sketch out his thoughts. To arrive at the bunker, one travels through a neat row of pear trees, palms, and palmettos, either orphaned or gifted to him through the years. He calls the green space "an accidental garden," converted from a parking lot when he purchased the property.

A natural forager, Holley honed his hunting skills in Bermondsey Market and Portobello Road, when he was living in London in his twenties. Motivated by the hunt, he scours estate sales, flea markets, and consignment stores wherever he travels in search of the rare and the rarefied for both his home and his clients'. His sharp eye can quickly survey an estate sale and discern if someone's velvet draperies lined with sumptuous silk can find new life draping the doorway of a narrow, moody hallway, or if a pair of 1940s Lucite candlesticks will meld with a disparate collection of bric-a-brac.

In his living room, such finds as a Forrest Moses painting—acquired for $200 at a charity resale shop—cozy up to a painted Chippendale chinoiserie-style vitrine and a pair of vintage Barcelona ottomans, which blend beautifully with a Belgian linen–covered banquette. "I don't think I have a decorative style," Holley says. "It's really about putting things together. It's not really styled, but a house filled with things I love that I've been carrying around for thirty years." There are touches of bold, unapologetic color. Treasures culled through the years form a playful menagerie where pricey items flirt with bargain-basement finds and where outdoor garden elements double as art, such as a chipped white-painted trellis behind a Louis XVI console. In the living room, a pair of oversized outdoor lanterns hangs above a lavish banquette casually strewn with vintage hand-embroidered pillows. With each new find, Holley's home will change again, whether by cosmic shift or a subtle rearrange.

opposite page Painted Chippendale vitrine in the chinoiserie style with interior upholstered in Fortuny. The piece is filled with Van Day Truex's rock-crystal candlesticks; two framed drawings by architect Emilio Terry; a white teapot with three spouts; and a yellow vase in the shape of wrapping paper by English artist Carol McNicoll. On the floor, an etching by Sir Frederick Leighton and a monoprint by Forrest Moses.

opposite In the library, three panels of a Victorian decoupage screen are mounted on the wall. An 1802 English Golden Square campaign piano, designed to be transported for an officer's use, serves here as a console. Jacob Collins' oil painting is from Meredith Long & Company. Lithograph by John Hoyland. The turn-of-the-century chair is in its original teal mohair with fringe. *above* The view from the hallway to the master bedroom, through portieres of vintage silk-velvet lined with a black-and-white cotton stripe. The bed is in front of a Chinese lacquered twelve-panel screen. *below* Console table with a base by Charles Masterson and painted top by English artist John Harwood. The oil painting is by artist Richard Gorman. Painting of trees is by Libbie Masterson.

opposite top In the living room, the banquette is upholstered in Belgian linen. A Duncan Phyfe oval English pedestal table serves as a dining table. The pair of Gustavian chairs is covered in a striped fabric by artist Rusty Arena. The Georgian chair is a copy and is upholstered in vintage hand-embroidered fabric. A French pier mirror is turned on its side; the crystal-and-gilt-bronze sconces are original to the mirror. Propped against the mirror are a framed offset lithograph by Robert Rauschenberg and a white-framed gouache-and-colored-pencil piece by Chad Sager, both from Devin Borden Hiram Butler Gallery. The large abstract painting is by Greg Lofgren. **opposite bottom right** In the music room, a birchwood cello rests beneath a Vose mahogany baby grand piano. **opposite bottom left** In an alcove, the French turn-of-the-century settee is part of a three-piece suite. The petite painted Louis XVI chair is covered in Clarence House's Dragon Empress fabric. The occasional table is a Moroccan piece. **above** In the red library is a set of Victorian decoupage screens found in London. Kenneth Noland oil painting, from Meredith Long & Company. A Louis XVI–reproduction daybed mixes with a mirrored '40s cocktail table. The English seventeenth-century armchair is covered with Osborne & Little multicolored check fabric. **right** On a staircase landing, a white-painted trellis enhances the Louis XVI console. The original Brno chair is upholstered in chocolate suede.

McKAY OTTO AND KEITH COFFEE

If living spaces are clues to attitude, then one of the most revealing environments of all must be an artist's. For painter McKay Otto, his coastal cottage serves up a perfect reflection of his work. It's an 1898 Victorian gingerbread, sited in a crumbling palm-lined neighborhood, just minutes from the Gulf of Mexico. Like his nylon-encased canvases with their pure-white palette, Otto's serene, seaside idyll, which he shares with partner Keith Coffee, is all about incandescent light, luminous spaces, and beckoning portals.

When Otto arrived at this charming setting years ago, the interiors of his double-decker bungalow were far from the airy rooms that one now glimpses. "I convinced my cousin to rent it to me. She exclaimed, astonished, "You want to live in that shack?" It was deplorable, with floors painted dark green, almost black, so as to not show the dirt; cheap, ugly brown paneling, which took five coats to cover; and a ghastly red kitchen." But Otto also saw something else—something more intrinsic: five hundred miles of sea breezes and light like Taos, where he once had a summer studio. "There's a sense of vastness here and of the infinite, which is what my work is all about," he says. He quotes one of his artistic inspirations, the late painter Agnes Martin, who was also a friend and mentor: "Agnes always said that it's about the light. And she told me that the light at the ocean is as beautiful as the high mountains."

Today, Otto's rooms have the pull of the past, balanced by the future—similar to the feeling one gets upon encountering a light installation by James Turrell, another of Otto's favorite contemporary artists. Antiques and estate finds cohabit with Otto's pure, abstract canvases here. The predominant pigment throughout is white: walls, woodwork, ceilings, even the floor, where his paint has splashed over the cream-colored boards and seagrass rugs. It suggests the inside of a seashell: nacreous, iridescent, aglow like mother-of-pearl. The studio space is the breakfast room at the front of the house, which faces the Gulf. The artist begins each day predawn, rising to walk the beach, where he scavenges the plastic objects that are often recycled in his canvases.

Most significantly, Otto credits his home by the sea with a transformation in his art-making. Before, his sculptures and the occasional painting series were dark, dark, dark. Otto layered graphite—the stuff of pencil leads—over canvases and sculptures alike. The effect was slightly depressing, recalling Rothko's later paintings: powerful but gloomy. Gone is the gloom; in its place, expansive light and whiteness emanate from these paintings and in turn echo throughout the cottage.

opposite Serving as studio and dining nook, this light-filled breakfast-room has paint-splattered seagrass rugs. The curtains screening this room from the bedchamber are bleached bed sheets. Between the tall windows, plastic lids from gallon buckets of gesso provide support for paintings.

opposite As befitting this Victorian-era bungalow, the bathroom testifies to the glories of late-nineteenth-century grooming, with a claw-footed tub, candlelit sconces salvaged from an old hotel, an antique pewter pitcher from Otto's grandmother's ranch, a marble mortar sans pestle and a Venetian Murano glass bowl. **above** A pair of industrial steel ladders offers access to the well-stocked art library. On the right, a futuristic expanse of white, Otto's *Untitled #2121T*. **right** An antique mahogany-cased baby grand holds center stage in the music room. Suspended from the ceiling are nineteenth-century gymnasts' rings, while an African tribal sculpture with embedded cowry shells stands guard.

opposite above left Art predominates in the sleeping space. Above the cotton-covered headboard is a Robert Motherwell lithograph from his "Flight" series, its sand-colored palette perfect for a seaside retreat. On the adjoining wall, Otto's ethereal monochrome *Untitled #2069U.* Beside the bed, a custom-designed, granite-topped dressing cabinet. ***opposite above right*** In a hall-way nook, an Eastlake marble-topped chest gets a coat of luminous pigment, echoing the orb-shaped canvases from Otto's "Infinity" series. The larger painting is *Untitled*. On the dresser: 19th-century Wedgwood candlesticks, a 1950s ceramic planter, a modernist lamp and an early Jim Beam bottle. ***opposite bottom*** This cozy sitting nook has a table concocted by placing wheels on an early wooden tailor's stand. The painting is *Untitled #2087I,* from Otto's "Cloud" series. ***above left*** The peeling facade of the second-floor porch barely hints at the light oasis inside. ***above right*** The kitchen, enlivened by a bold dose of chartreuse, is the sole exception to the white-on-white harmony. Over the pantry door is an oil portrait, *Inez Otto*, by artist Betty Mobley. The concept of exposed cabinets was inspired by a visit to Donald Judd's house in Marfa, Texas. ***left*** A jolt of white in the entrance that's also an informal gallery for Otto's ongoing creations. An early twentieth-century wooden church pew contrasts with Otto's monochrome paintings. Early twentieth-century Thonet bentwood armchair.

SALLE WERNER-VAUGHN

Once upon five follies, artist Salle Werner-Vaughn rescued a quintet of row houses to form a very personal commune she named "Harmonium." With a twirl of hair bundled in a loose knot atop her head and her fondness for fairy tales, she can remind you of the chicest schoolmarm ever. Her abstract paintings, which sometimes scale three to four times the size of her small frame, spin mythical and dreamy tales. Her art is in the collections of such distinguished museums as the Metropolitan Museum of Art in New York, the Museum of Fine Arts, Boston, and the Museum of Fine Arts, Houston, as well as private collections around the globe. The ethereal abstractions appear hazy with an otherworldly sense of color, from a frost of azure blue to a blast of light-filled yellow—works that evolve out of an admitted concern with time.

Like many creative beings, Vaughn seeks refuge far from the world beyond her threshold. She finds peace and solitude in a dreamy cottage called "Elsewhere"—one of five diminutive painted clapboard homes built early in the last century (between 1905 and 1920) and lovingly saved, one by one, from certain demise. Although she resides with her mathematician husband in a stately home in a classic neighborhood several miles away, she often invites guests to hole up here, beneath the attic studio where she paints each day. Within the walls of her compound, Vaughn has painstakingly leveled, sanded, and painted the old plank wood floors, replaced crumbling walls, and retooled the plumbing and electricity.

Vaughn never intended to make it her mission to breathe new life into these worn, tattered structures, which she has rechristened "Now and Then," "Here and There," "Elsewhere," "By the Way," and "Clouds." Quite the contrary, it was all a matter of happenstance. Months after she finished buffing and puffing her first life-sized dollhouse, the interior was pretty as a picture—too pretty, in fact, to risk dribbling paint across the celadon- and chartreuse-patterned painted floors. Too pretty to worry about spilling turpentine on her precious eighteenth-century French and Italian antiques thoughtfully scattered about the old homestead. Vaughn eventually acquired another cottage nearby, then another next door, and another down the road, and finally another—each more suitable than the last. Each perfect for whittling the days away, happily painting.

"I see each house as a novella, and the vignettes set inside each of them are the medium in which my story is told," Vaughn says. "To me they appear romantic, nostalgic and theatrical. Everything I choose has a meaning. Nothing is idly arranged. I try within these walls to create a perfect universe where everything is about harmony. Here you have the fluid versus the orderly geometric, arm-wrestling each other."

opposite In a guest chamber, an antique French painted daybed. The eighteenth-century-style bergère, made during the nineteenth century, is covered in a Chinese silk fabric. The period gilt frame holds one of Vaughn's works. The oil painting above the daybed is also by Vaughn.

opposite The painted backdrop is a scene from an opera produced at the Paris Opera House around the turn of the century. The bed, believed to be eighteenth-century French, is upholstered in raw silk. The frame in the corner is one of many period Italian, Spanish and French frames Vaughn began collecting years ago to display on their own or with her artwork. *above* A room inside "Here and There" is awash in blues. An Italian gilt torchère holds an iron goddess head. In the background, one of Vaughn's works: a large mirror painted with Revlon's Cherries in the Snow lip color in a jigsaw-puzzle pattern. *above right* The windows in a bedroom, draped with loose white sheeting both for privacy and to filter the harsh rays of the sun, showcase dreamy cast shadows of the foliage outside. *right* In an unexpected punch of pattern, Vaughn wallpapered a sitting room with Rose Cummings' bold hunter-green striped wallpaper. The stairs in the background lead to the artist's studio nest in the second-floor attic.

opposite The long gallery was once three small rooms. The floor, designed and painted by Vaughn, was inspired by an amalgam of ancient floor designs. Propped against the wall, just one of Vaughn's many massive canvases. The settee, draped in raw silk, was made in Belgium. **above** A bedroom is filled with slipcovered furniture. The bed is a painted Austrian antique. By the window is a dress form from the couturier Charles James. **below** The sunny sitting room is filled with various gilt treasures.

ANGIE BARRETT

If you've ever been inside a space that utterly resonates with its inhabitant, you already know how it goes. Door swings open. Vista unfolds. Your eye skips around the room, and you blurt to your host, "This place looks just like you!" That's what a great inner sanctum should be, anyway; what's the point if it doesn't reflect the true you? And that's how it goes at Angie Barrett's. There is strong art. There are tart colors. There are books laser-cut into the shapes of pistols. Like Barrett says about the electrified word "Vicious" hanging in her bedroom, "It's not for everybody."

In fact, this gutsy interior is a tweaked new guise for an already opulent house. Since the name "Barrett" went on the deed in 1994—the house has changed hands precious few times — it has brimmed with top-drawer furniture, rugs, finishes, and flourishes; a grand place, propped with glamorous things, all wrapped in a soothing palette. But since Barrett's life is ever changing, you could surmise that her environs had to follow.

Enter decorator James McInroe. As Barrett tells it, it all started innocently enough. Then the redecoration spark turned blowtorch. Barrett, true to character, is fearless. McInroe, true to character, isn't known for quiet interiors. Put the two together, and batten down the hatches. A brave acidic green coats the family room, a 1970s addition, pre-Barrett. A patterned carpet à la David Hicks was unfurled below. On top of that went some rather wild juxtapositions: stools upholstered in cheetah hide, a pair of '50s Italian club chairs in hairy white cowhide, and a 1980s glass-and-steel Brueton coffee table. You get the idea. This occurred all over the house, this rearranging, recovering, remixing, replacing, all heightened by liberal doses of McInroe's trademark acerbic hues.

Barrett stepped up the art program, too. There's now a Schnabel over a fireplace, a Currin in a front hall and two Thomas Struths. There's a Kippenberger and a Glenn Brown. Another thrill? Books. Hundreds of them, many first editions, all over the place. Barrett hunts for them everywhere, and she has rare-book dealers scouring, too. On just one shelf in one room are tomes on Hiro, van Dyck, Basquiat, Warhol, Poiret, and Phil Stern. There are books on design, art, architecture, photography, and fashion, fashion, fashion. And, if you visit twice, they'll probably have been rearranged. Barrett loves them and works on them until the wee hours. She orders clear Mylar for them, too, and covers them herself. "I'm hooked. That's what I do till 2 a.m.," she says. "It's therapy!"

opposite In a corner of a guest bedroom, a lioness rug, circa 1930s, a Napoleon III–style settee, a 1930s glass floor lamp and a rare Paul Frankl dresser. The bronze-and-mirror coffee table is 1940s French.

opposite In the lounge area of Angie Barrett's bedroom is the work *Vicious*, 1999, by British artists Tim Noble and Sue Webster. James McInroe–designed love seat in Henry Calvin fabric. Mirrored coffee table by Nancy Corzine. Fanciful Murano glass chandelier. *above* For the sunroom side of the cavernous great room, McInroe had 1950s Robsjohn-Gibbings chairs covered in orange-melon velvet with Greek-key fabric tape trim. The Saarinen table is vintage Knoll, and the Murano glass chandelier is 1930s. *below* In a corner lounge, a club chair (foreground left) by T.H. Robsjohn-Gibbings for John Widdicomb, in a David Hicks fabric by Lee Jofa. The charcoal mohair sofa is a James McInroe design; pillows are David Hicks linen from Lee Jofa. Steel-and-mirror coffee table is mid-century French. Goatskin rug. *following pages* The living room with its Louis XVI–style settee, and late 1940s Italian chairs in apple-green Brunschwig & Fils velvet. The table lamp is 1950s Venetian glass, the plaster torchière is French 1930s. The lattice screen is '50s French. Over the fireplace, a Julian Schnabel broken-plate painting, *I Remember Udnie Too*, from 1988. The right side of the face is artist Francesco Clemente; the left is artist Ross Bleckner. Barrett has met Bleckner and Schnabel; she's working on Clemente.

BILL MACKIN

You'll swear we've had one too many martinis when we report that the dwelling you see here is mere steps away from a busy avenue—hustle, bustle, stoplights, street life, authentic taquerias. But hiding in a thicket behind it all, in a tucked-away neighborhood, is the most sophisticated lake house ever seen in the midst of a metropolis. Welcome to Bill Mackin's mental vacation—one he gets to take every day, the lucky devil.

Mackin's place is neither French nor Italian nor Tudor nor Zen. No faux about it. Just one look at the handsome, angular house—built by Texas architect Harris Kemp for himself, in 1942—and it's easy to understand why Mackin fell for it. Mr. Mackin, you see, as creative director of Neiman Marcus' home and gift galleries nationwide, moves in the manic design world, so a house with calming effects is key. (After a day of advising buyers and boarding planes and soaking up trade shows and analyzing trends and crunching numbers, you'd need a break, too.) Mackin may speak softly and is nothing if not genteel, but his brain is stuck in overdrive. Comes with the territory: He loves hunting and gathering and learning. Another trait of his? The Eye: that rare gift for understanding shape, color, proportion and line, and an inherent knack for knowing how to display it all, masterfully. In the kitchen, stacks of artisan plates. In the living room, a squadron of incense-burning porcelain parrots. In his bedroom, a clean-lined, black-and-white teacart from Yugoslavia, serving up richly colored Blenko glass vessels. Mackin's curatorial cunning makes for a tasty mix: souvenirs from travels, props from stores, favorite furniture, all resonating in this peaceful, ivory shell—a shell that took him nearly a year to rescue and refine from botched previous renovations, freeing it from what he calls its "bondage of glass bricks and bad siding." Out went an odd third bedroom squeezed between the other two; in went shimmering bronze-mesh screens across the sleeping porch. Out went ill-fitting storm windows; in went tiny slate tiles across the dining-room floor. Mackin even tore down bad walls and worse windows that had enclosed a former breezeway, now the sexiest outdoor "room" in town, wrapped on the street side in chain-link fencing and left thrillingly open on the other. In fact, after Mackin's deft magic, all of the house's cabin-like cues are celebrated: grooved wooden walls inside and out, an honest little galley kitchen now brimming with stainless-steel fittings, and those generous windows—some of which retract to the side, opening the living room to a porch—onto all that leafy green out back. Repeat: lucky devil.

opposite Bill Mackin mixes a 1940s Paul Frankl cork-topped cocktail table with a Randolph & Hein slipcovered sofa, 1920s rug, Scandinavian floor lamp, and a dramatic, cinematic Lorraine Tady painting.

opposite The upstairs sleeping porch spans the length of the house; Mackin installed screens of bronze mesh—the subtle, honey-colored shimmer in the sunlight is unforgettable. *above* The back of Bill Mackin's circa-1942 "cabin in the city" by architect Harris Kemp. *below* Mackin furnishes the outdoor breezeway as a luxurious living room. The sofa and chairs were designed by Charles Pfister for Knoll, and the floor lamps are by T.H. Robsjohn-Gibbings. The twist columns were Randolph Hearst's, collected when he was building his famous castle.

opposite Mackin's bedroom, with its showstopping bed of black walnut, made in England, one of an edition of eight. Cocktail tables by Florence Knoll serve as night stands; one holds an early 1980s torso by an English sculptor. The two framed works are by artist Lorraine Tady. On the bed, a craft quilt and needlepoint pillows, one handmade by Mackin. *above* A collection of Fornasetti plates and glassware. The painting is by modernist Toni LaSelle. *below* Jens Risom's 1941 chairs for Knoll elevated from their usual fabric webbing to leather, circle a Saarinen table.

ROB BRINKLEY

I blame it all on Buffy and Jody. My longtime urge to live sky-high came from those two, whom I watched on television in *Family Affair*, coming and going from their Uncle Bill's handsome high-rise apartment in New York, complete with sparkly views and an English butler. (I especially coveted that last bit.) For a kid growing up in a little Mayberry of a town in northern Kentucky, the thought of taking an elevator up to one's apartment was wildly, madly exciting. So when, as an adult who'd made it to a different big city but a big city nonetheless, I began hunting for a domicile, I thought about little Buffy and Jody and their views and their butler. Why not, I thought. Carpe diem.

That was seven years ago, and I'm still riding elevators. Every night, I park in the subterranean garage of my modernist building, circa 1963, and ride twenty-three stories up to my tiny little penthouse. But there's no English butler to greet me. Instead, it's an odd assemblage of art, chairs, and books. I began collecting chairs in 1988, when I saw a tall, elegant, ladder-back stunner being uncrated as a prop for the couture salon of a department store. That chair changed everything. I began to think of seating as sculpture, not just something on which to perch. So when a twin to that beautiful object—a Hill House chair, designed in 1902 by the Scottish architect Charles Rennie Mackintosh—presented itself, I bought it. No turning back. Next was a Wassily chair by Marcel Breuer, then an Eames, then a Bertoia. I immersed myself in midcentury, then veered toward the Bauhaus, then tiptoed into the Memphis movement. Chairs are now wedged into my closets, ringing my office, and "visiting" the homes of some very accommodating friends. The ones I keep close to me seem to have something in common, a certain precision of line. I can't pick a favorite. Around me, I have the works of Mies van der Rohe (several), Mackintosh (three), Le Corbusier (ditto), Eileen Gray, Ettore Sottsass, and Franco Albini. At the urging of another good friend—she complained that there was nowhere to actually *sit*—I've stirred in one sofa and some tables.

But you've no doubt noticed the books. I like chairs, I like books. I like books about chairs. And, if you peruse my bookcases and piles, I suppose I also like Rolls-Royces, Marlene Dietrich, Adirondack cabins, Queen Elizabeth II, Slim Aarons, and New York. And while there may not be a Mr. French bustling about the apartment, ironing my newspapers and laying out my clothes, when I sit in my chairs and thumb through my books, I do love my life in the sky. I occasionally think about Buffy and Jody, too. They were cool, but I have better furniture.

opposite This first-generation Charles and Ray Eames lounge chair, in original leather, was designed in 1960 for the lobby of the Time-Life Building in New York. The carved-head iron coatrack is antique; the stool is African. The configurable teak wall unit is stamped "Made in Denmark" on each piece.

opposite top The living room features a pair of Eileen Gray Transat chairs by Ecart, 1927; a pair of rare brown-suede Knoll club chairs by Mies van der Rohe from late 1920s; and a sofa by Charles Pfister for Knoll, 1971. The Memphis-like lacquered cocktail table is one of a pair, bought at a thrift-store sidewalk sale. Propped against the wall is a work by Victor Vasarely. *opposite bottom right* The green Wellington boots are a signs of an obsession with the British countryside. (They are typically tossed in the back of the old Range Rover, just in case.) *opposite bottom left* A detail of the bedroom shows an English blanket of red wool and a vintage floor lamp from a hospital-supply company. *right* A 1960s Olivetti Praxis 48 typewriter, designed by Ettore Sottsass. *below* In the bedroom are books, books, books— and an Ettore Sottsass lounge chair in which to read them, designed in 1983 for Knoll. The articulated floor lamp is 1980s; the framed abstract is titled *Fetal Duck II*. *below right* Books for reading and a Danish phone—in MoMA's permanent collection—for talking.

opposite The dining room features original Mies van der Rohe Brno chairs—in their original leather—by Gratz Industries, the New York company that worked with Mies directly to first manufacture his furniture in the States. The Parsons table is a gift from a friend, who used it in the workroom of her fashion company. It holds a rather scientific-looking collection of Pyrex and a jumbo transistor tube. Overhead is a favorite fixture of the Memphis movement: an Aurora pendant lamp by Flos, found in a consignment shop. In the background right is a Charles Rennie Mackintosh D.S.3 chair, designed in 1918 and made by Cassina. ***above*** Another living-room view. The low bowl on the cocktail table is by Alvar Aalto, designed in 1937. The curved teak bowl on the Danish wall unit is by Jens Quistgaard for Dansk. The shaped canvas is by artist Paul Lewis. In front of it is another Mackintosh chair, this one the Argyle, designed in 1897 and made by Cassina. ***right*** Above a Franco Albini chair for Knoll, 1949, now in the Knoll Museum, is a slow-shutter, hand-colored photograph by Reinhard Ziegler, taken from a moving vehicle.

DANA HARPER

A few years ago, artist Dana Harper's heart was swept away by a beauty: a multilevel modernist marvel designed in 1958 by Harwood Taylor, of the architecture firm Neuhaus & Taylor. Harper fell hard for the house, which was in desperate need of a head-to-toe makeover. He saw through the disarray of a bungled renovation (abandoned halfway through, no less) and recognized a stunner with good bones perched on a lot that sloped gently down to a bayou. But the lady needed some work. Enter the firm of Stern and Bucek Architects, which had just completed the restoration of the 1951 Phillip Johnson–designed de Menil house, commissioned by the late John and Dominique de Menil. Architect Bill Stern considers Harper's house to be among Taylor's finest, and he suspects that Taylor, along with other notable architects of the time, may have been influenced by Johnson's design for the de Menils. In its day, Harper's house had been a well-known bit of architecture; it had been published but subsequently forgotten and neglected. Had Harper had not stepped in, it would most likely have been torn down.

After he purchased it, Harper contemplated what to do. "I didn't do anything right away," he says. "I just spent time at the house and thought about it. Then I tracked down drawings, family photographs of the house, as well as historical documentation from magazines." The original family had sold the property in the late 1970s, and it had fallen into the hands of its second owners, who had other ideas for it. Among them: painting white all the brick, inside and out, as well as the rich walnut veneer paneling; lowering the coffered ceiling and replacing it with flat sheetrock; removing the original kitchen and ripping out the turquoise St. Charles steel cabinetry system; and gutting the master bath, including the sunken terrazzo tub. The gardens, pool deck and courtyard? They had been destroyed—completely.

Undeterred, Stern and Bucek and their client took the spatially complex house back to its heyday. To be accurate, this was not a straight restoration. The architects and homeowner restored much of what the house had been, then tweaked it for modern living. They water-blasted the paint off the bricks; replaced the white-painted paneling with new walnut veneer; installed a new roof with the four-ply, coal-tar material originally used; rebuilt the beautiful coffered ceilings, framing them with channels of light; and restored the original terrazzo-style bathtub. The kitchen was damaged beyond repair, and while the new one pays homage to the old, it actually works more successfully in the twenty-first century. But like most houses, this modernist masterpiece is still a work in progress.

opposite Black-walnut paneling lines the east wall of the family room and conceals the entry to a full bar and guest bath. A Vladimir Kagan sofa pulls up to a retro cocktail table and an Eero Saarinen end table from Knoll. The woven-wicker stools are by Franco Albini.

opposite The oil painting in the family room was created by Harper's mother, Lillie Cullen. The red upholstered sofa is custom-made, the rug is antique Persian, the pair of rattan chairs is by Poul Kjaerholm. **above** The Harper house, shot here from the back, was designed in 1960. **below** In the dining room, circa-1970 Castelli chairs surround a Saarinen marble-topped table from Knoll. The hanging fixture was made in Italy in the early 1950s. The candy-necklace sculpture in the kitchen is by Paul Kittelson, from Barbara Davis Gallery

opposite top In the corner of the master bedroom is a flag-liner iron chair, created in 1950 by Hans J. Wegner. On the cigarette table are pieces of Czech and Italian glass. The enameled-metal table was inspired by Jean Prouvé; the groovy resin lamp, circa 1970, was a junk-store find. ***opposite bottom*** Surrounding the Hans Bellman Popsicle table in the brick-lined breakfast nook are original Eames stainless Eiffel Tower chairs with turquoise bikini pads—an homage to the turquoise St. Charles kitchen that once stood in the space. Vintage glass chandelier. The chartreuse tabletop pieces are part of a collection of Russel Wright's American Modern ceramics. ***above*** A vintage Nelson pendant hangs above the sunken conversation area in the living room. Harper inherited the burled-wood cocktail table from his grandparents. ***left*** In the master bedroom, the bedspread was custom-created by Lori Cassady from a template designed by the homeowners. The pillows and linens were crafted from vintage material from the 1960s. The black-and-white striped vase is a replica of a Cubist piece designed by Pavel Janák. The bronze deer-head sculpture is by Ken Little.

DON CONNELLY

When store owner and interior designer Don Connelly turned forty, he bought the farm, so to speak. Instead of having an unfortunate midlife meltdown, he bought a pickup truck and hit the country roads. "I've wanted a farm my whole life," he says. "I realized on my fortieth birthday, 'Okay, if you live to be eighty, you're lucky. This is midway; if you don't do it at midway, it's never going to happen.' So I just made it a goal and said, 'Now is the time. Go find it and buy it.'"

Eventually he found an eighty-acre farm in cow country. When you're seated on a rattan chaise on the porch, all you can see for miles are scenic pastures. One neighbor has about four hundred acres, another has two hundred, and another, three hundred, granting the fortunate Connelly twenty-mile unobstructed views. "That's what drew me to this," he says. "My life Monday to Friday is so busy with people that this is my retreat. I come here and turn my phone off. The man that was helping me restore the house said, 'Where do you want your phone jack?' And I said, 'I don't.'"

Finding this farm may have been a formidable task, but restoring the 918-square-foot, barely standing farmhouse was monumental. "The farmhouse had probably not been painted in thirty or forty years," Connelly says. "And it had not been lived in for over thirty years, according to the neighbors….It's on pier-and-beam, and the piers were rotted underneath, so it was leaning over to one side." The house was filled with old furniture with springs popping out, and its windows had long been shot out. "It looked like something out of *Gunsmoke*, but I saw potential." Connelly quickly constructed a barn-red guesthouse (which today sleeps eight) just down a stone path to serve as temporary living quarters, and for the next two years he renovated the main house and grounds. The first project was a pool. Next came a wraparound porch, screened in on the back side and doubling as a sleeping porch. A new barn built of old materials was erected as a home for the horses. Out went the outhouse; up went a chicken coop. Rounding out the rural redo were custom iron-framed windows and doors throughout the house, an expanded tin roof, and a bathroom, which necessitated the first plumbing inside the structure.

Connelly filled his farmstead with furniture he'd stored away when downsizing his city digs several years ago. Add to that bric-a-brac from Paris flea markets and finds from local antiques shows, and Connelly's country retreat was complete. On weekends or whenever he has time for a quick getaway, he piles into his pickup, two small dogs in tow, and heads to his country house to commune with the cows, chickens, wild turkeys, peacocks, guinea fowl, horses, and a rescued farm dog named Mikey.

opposite The circa-1950 horn chair in the living room originally decorated a hotel lobby in Barcelona. The footstool, also Spanish, is covered with goatskin. The pencil drawing by artist Michael Collins is titled *Adam and Eve*. The dog portrait and shell tramp-art basket were found in the South of France.

preceding pages The dining table was found at an antique shop for $75. The old French leather dining chairs are missing a fourth, so Connelly pulls up a cowhide-covered antique French ottoman. An Italian overscaled reproduction of the *Mona Lisa*. **opposite left** Curiosities in the living room include ostrich-egg lamps, created by Connelly, atop a nineteenth-century French Louis-Philippe commode with stained, stripped finish. A 1930s French leather smoking chair is paired with a deer footstool. The eighteenth-century wooden shield with crucifix was carried back on a trip from Guatemala. **above** In the master bedroom, the simple farm table, a flea-market find, holds a collection of stuffed turtles and wild-bird eggs that took two decades to accumulate. The black-and-beige striped headboard is hand-painted. **below left** In the kitchen, a Scottish hunter's trophy behind glass contains about two dozen kinds of bird claws. Below, a 1920s American Indian Pueblo vessel atop a rustic butcher block perches on an old farm table. **below right** In the dining room, an amazing collection of dried wasps' nests and shed snakeskins adorn a French garden statue of a stag. The oil painting is nineteenth-century Italian renaissance.

KAY O'TOOLE

In Kay O'Toole's life, worlds don't collide; they meld together seamlessly. By day, this antiquarian with a penchant for eighteenth- and nineteenth-century French and Italian furnishings fills her eponymous antiques store with hand-picked treasures—fragile creamware, crusty crystal chandeliers, muslin-covered settees trimmed in faded gilt, Venetian mirrors, and the like. The combination of gray, beige, and white soothes the eyes and calms the soul. At dusk, she returns to her high-rise home to unlock a door onto a world that perfectly reflects the one she just left behind.

An inveterate collector of everything from Madonnas and their vermeil crowns to creamware plates and delicate, antique monogrammed linens, O'Toole has assembled the best bits from the past centuries into wildly eccentric interiors. A hunter and gatherer by nature, she scours flea markets in Paris and the Côte d'Azur, returning with beautiful pieces. Some she bravely parts with; others, she simply cannot. "I love drama," she says. "I think that you shouldn't have things just to fill a space but that those things should contribute to the mood and should be something you respond to. For instance, you should look for a table that stirs something in you, not just look for a table because you need a table."

Merging two high-rise apartments into one gracious space, O'Toole created an open concept with few walls to divide the area, save for the two wings that house her bedroom, baths, and guest room. A chalky shade of Gustavian gray unifies the space, a color chosen to simplify the task of coordinating pieces, fabrics, and paint as much as for its appeal. But O'Toole is most at home living with a bit of imperfection. Peely paint, pitted mirrors, chipped gilt, and faded Fortuny all endear themselves. The mottled kitchen wall behind the baker's rack? There's nothing faux here—that effect resulted when some aged wallpaper was removed, leaving behind a remnant of glue. Two dove-gray chairs upholstered in fragile kid leather seemed… well, too pristine for O'Toole's taste, so she darkened and roughed them up a bit with leather polish.

Glorious to look at, and undoubtedly to live in, this home is all about the details. To quickly stride past a pair of stags' heads hung on a plastered wall is to miss the fact that they're not impeccable taxidermy but intricate lifelike, wood-carved replicas. To brush by the bulbous buffet and not take the time to inspect it is to miss out on the discovery that it's not a single bow-front chest, but two corner cabinets simply pushed together. Every nook and cranny is filled with glorious eighteenth- and nineteenth-century treasures, each with a history all its own.

opposite The black-painted bookcase, circa 1800, was made in France in the japonaise style; running along its sides are Japanese scenes as the French envisioned them. Above the bookcase are a gilt mirror and a pair of iron sconces fitted with Fortuny shades, all eighteenth-century Italian. The eighteenth-century walnut side chairs are also covered in Fortuny.

opposite top The late-1800s sofa, in the style of Napoleon III, is covered in a dove-gray cotton O'Toole had specially quilted. The white-and-yellow papier-mâché columns are two of six found in an architectural salvage shop. *opposite bottom* In the living room are a Louis XVI French settee, an oil painting of Saint Catherine of France, and a French Napoleon III side chair; a French eighteenth-century Louis XVI carved and painted chair and a cigarette table from Italy hold court. To the left are architectural fragments and a stone lawn ball. *above* In O'Toole's bedroom is an iron four-poster bed of her own design, crafted by artisan Bill Peck. The coverlet and curtains are Fortuny. *left* In the living room are a French eighteenth-century daybed and a Venetian street lamp transformed into a floor lamp. *following page right* O'Toole's dining room could be dubbed the Fortuny room: The curtains and upholstery are both vintage Fortuny, the screen propped in the corner is covered in a tattered piece of the Italian fabric, and the walls are mottled with a parchment glaze that mimics the pattern. The eighteenth-century fruitwood buffet was made in France in the "chocolate slab" style—so called because the front panels resemble scored chocolate bar. *following page left* In the living room, an old iron lattice garden table holds a plaster head, a collection of Madonna crowns, an eighteenth-century wooden saint's hand, and a dyed-ivory bluebird figurine.

LISA AND KING GROSSMAN

You could call it a midlife change—not a crisis, really, because there was nothing "we have to take our life in a new direction, stat!" about it. But when in-demand decorator J. Randall Powers received a call from his new clients, Lisa and King Grossman, they told him they wanted to wipe the proverbial design slate clean (six years in a traditional Georgian) and start fresh. On the hunt for a new house, the couple was ready to settle on a Spanish-style house that was under construction. Then one day their design direction changed to a pristine, modern dwelling that architect Allen Bianchi had designed around a magnificent old oak tree with limbs that majestically shade the backyard like a natural canopy. The couple put in an offer, and soon it was theirs. There was only one catch: They feared the trappings of their old life wouldn't mesh with the next chapter of their lives—modern living. Fortunately they contacted the right designer. J. Randall Powers has inspired many homeowners to leave their past behind and start anew.

Of this particular couple, Powers says, "They didn't play follow the leader by wanting things that they had seen before. And they didn't want Europe brought back to America. They have diverse tastes and like things a bit mixed up. A much more American aesthetic." One request from the Grossmans was a plasma television in the living room. Such an appeal sends many designers into a catatonic state, but let's admit it: Most of us want one, whether or not we're willing to cop to it. Cleverly, Powers did not hide or disguise the TV, but made it a highlight of the room. He encased it in dark wenge-wood paneling that extends up to the sleek cement-faced fireplace. Beneath it, a silk mohair-covered banquette runs from wall to hearth with a seating area composed of antique chairs, goatskin-covered stools, and cigarette tables. "I wanted it to be sexy," Powers says.

Then he started the Grossmans on the path to collecting iconic pieces from some of the biggest names in decorating. A 1940s-era Venini chandelier hangs in the dining room; other acquisitions include a plaster Giacometti lamp that stood in the Yves Saint Laurent boutique in Paris in the '70s; Klismos chairs; Wicker Works balustrade glass tables; and Frances Rogers's Kalef Alaton–designed lapis table. In the works for the entry: a massive bronze lantern, designed in the spirit of Giacometti by Powers and Carole Vitale, which will be patinated in chalky white. Ultimately, Powers brought the pair to the point where collecting well—and living well—within a modern mind-set suits them perfectly.

opposite In the dining room are Klismos silver-leaf-backed dining chairs by Wicker Works, a pair of Sud benches by Christian Liaigre for Holly Hunt, and a custom Macassar ebony Solstice dining table from Manheim-Ruseau. The chandelier is antique Venini Murano glass, from John Gregory Studios. Abstract painting by Esteban Vicente is from McClain Gallery.

preceding pages The homeowners insisted that a plasma-screen television be mounted in the living room. Powers' solution: to inset the device in a paneled wall of wenge wood. Sconces by Jean de Merry. Custom banquette covered in silk mohair. Custom Mercer cigarette tables from Dessin Fournir. Suede-and-pony-hair stools from Mariana Antinori. Pair of Swedish neoclassical armchairs by Therien. *opposite above* The Rose Tarlow lacewood Art Deco–style desk in the hall is a copy of one that belonged to Hollywood mogul David Geffen. The white plaster lamp is an original Diego Giacometti for Jean-Michel Frank. Bronze Diego Giacometti stool covered in lambskin. Cy Twombly set of works on paper entitled *Five Greek Poets and a Philosopher*. *opposite bottom right* Christian Liaigre for Holly Hunt Outremer bed. Leather, nail-head-studded side table with a Saladino-style glass lamp. *opposite bottom left* In the living room, a chocolate-brown leather-upholstered chaise was the single piece the couple brought to their new contemporary home. Elizabeth Peyton etching, from McClain Gallery, is on a custom Lucite stand. *above left* In the entry, a Carrara marble–topped, twenty-two karat white gold–leafed console table designed by J. Randall Powers, and an Andy Moses abstract from McClain Gallery. The smaller painting, propped on a Lucite easel, is by Marco Villegas, from Meredith Long & Co. Barbara Barry for Baker ottoman covered in orange-colored leather. *above right* In the master bedroom, one of a diptych commissioned from artist Angelina Nasso through McClain Gallery. The custom-upholstered bed is in Mokum Texiles linen. *right* In the master bath, Wicker Works' classic glass baluster table and an Art Deco ivory-inlaid and Macassar ebony chair.

AMIS and GUILLAUME GARRIGUE

Guillaume Garrigue is rather used to going in circles. His driveway is one. His living room is one. His bed? You guessed it. Garrigue's world is a whirl—of arcs, curves, circles, and undulations, courtesy of Oklahoma architect Bruce Goff and the forward-thinking man who originally commissioned this habitable work of art, an importer-exporter of giftware and decorative accessories. Key word: decorative. For here at this house, there are thousands of tiles, walls fashioned from Frankoma pottery, tiny eighteen-karat-gold-dipped blocks running rampant amid acres of rosewood, walnut, cypress, and mahogany. There are circles punched out of stone walls, sliding panels made of sparkly Higgins glass, and wood panels galore, with off-kilter seams and grooves. Living here, confirms Garrigue, "is like living in an art piece."

Even the arrival sequence is far, far out of the ordinary. The Round House, as it is known, welcomes you under the shelter of a hundred-foot-diameter steel cage dome that drips with pale purple wisteria. Ease your car onto the circular driveway—completely enclosed by the dome—and you are already "inside" an outdoor room. Such is the beauty of Goff's trademark blurring of boundaries— what has been called a "freedom from convention," an "intellectual abandon." Abandon as in wild, which is how things really get once you step onto the circular pads that float above a fish pond and push through two hinged portals in a curved wall made of Frankoma tiles. Which way to go from there? Maybe it's straight ahead, into the sunken conversation pit anchored by a soaring, trumpet-shaped copper fireplace hood that descends from a huge oval skylight. Go left and you're headed to-ward the dining area and kitchen, skirting a curved wall of stone punctuated with artist-made discs of brightly colored resin. Even the bathrooms here are not bathrooms, but stone grottoes, with ornately detailed ceilings of wood and eighteen-karat tiles—the same gold tiles that zoom and race around the place, sometimes in single rows, sometimes doubled up.

Goff was clearly having fun—but not at the expense of the house itself. It is overbuilt, with a steel-cage infrastructure, self-cleaning heating and air-conditioning systems, even its own cooling tower. Progressive stuff for 1957 to 1962, the time it took for top craftsmen and artists to execute this manic, organic work—a work that is, by design, not for everyone. It is certainly for Garrigue, a photographer/director who bought the house in 2004 with his wife, Amis, a handbag and accessories designer. "It is," he says, "a surrounding *full* of eye candy."

opposite The sunken conversation pit, dominated by a shimmering hammered-copper fireplace hood. The Eames walnut stools are original to the house; the sunburst carpeting is a re-creation of architect Bruce Goff's original design. The tiled bar, background left, is fully cantilevered.

opposite Sliding panels by Higgins Glass Studio, right, open the lounge to the sunken conversation area. The Suzanne chairs are by Japanese architect Kazuhide Takahama, designed in 1965 for Gavina. The telescoping Pipistrello lamp is a late 1960s design by Gae Aulenti for Martinelli Luce. In the background is the Round House's stunning front wall of glass and Frankoma pottery. *above* A side of the Round House, showing the structure's curvilinear shape. *below* A garden gate bears the mosaics that also feature heavily throughout the house.

above Goff's open-plan dining space features a built-in buffet. Beyond the stone wall—punctured with circles—is the kitchen. The dramatic wooden beams that "pierce" the wall each have their own built-in lighting at the tips. The dining chairs are Mies van der Rohe's woven-cane model MR10, designed in 1927. Overhead is Poul Christiansen's hand-folded plastic Le Klint lamp, from 1971.
below The mirrored master bedroom of the Round House features—what else—a round bed. The bedcover is a replica of the original. Behind the pillows, a curved, built-in tiled table contains flip-up storage compartments and the master control for the house's original speaker system. The Chinese characters around the bed's base double as gigantic drawer pulls.

above The view from the den/lounge toward the central, circular living space, complete with a generous, sunken conversation pit, that makes up the hub of the floor plan. The gently arced stone wall at left is punctuated by discs of colored resin. Triangular panels of wood embellish the ceiling—and often the walls—on this main level of the house. *below left* The entry hall in 2002. *below right* The walk-in master bath—which has no door—is grotto-like with walls of river rock. Circular white tiles cover the fascia of the curved counter and the sink bowls below the countertop.

JAN AND KA YEUNG

At the end of any given photo shoot, stylist Jan Yeung has been known to say, "Come over for our lychee martinis!" If you take her up on the invitation, you get to go inside one of Dallas' most famous midcentury high-rises, then up to the third floor. And when the dramatic, red-orange door—decorated with black Chinese characters that beckon "good fortune"—to her apartment swings open, you will likely find her husband, photographer Ka Yeung, on the other side. He will be very glad to see you. And he will most certainly be smiling. So cheerful and centered are the Yeungs that you quickly come to expect a lot of this grinning and beaming. And they do a lot of it here, in their treetop apartment in a 1957 building designed by legendary Texas architect Howard Meyer, who devised a pinwheel-shaped plan for the edifice, which allows for windows on three sides of most apartments, a highly uncommon perk for a high-rise dwelling.

Meyer would've loved the Yeungs, who deftly mix the modern with the marvelous inside his project. In the living room, a pair of rare Hans Wegner lounge chairs shares the limelight with a long, lean George Nakashima table. Over here, a knobby little tree trunk of a table. Over there, the chicest rosewood settee you've ever seen. In the dining room, a Danish wall unit (another Wegner) faces off to a Le Corbusier dining table, relieved of its usual clear-glass top for a long, rectangular wood top that's been decoupaged by Ka with pages from Chinese almanacs. Personalization is a theme here, beginning with the space itself. The Yeungs chucked the previous owner's wall mirrors, bright green carpet, leopard-print wallpaper, and plastic parquet floors. They reconfigured walls in the sleeping quarters and, more importantly, reclaimed the original outdoor terrace. (Somewhere along the way, the terrace had been glassed in, masking the inside view of the building's trademark sunscreens, concrete grids à la Mondrian that hang over the windows and terraces, minimizing sun damage while dappling the interior with intriguing light patterns throughout the day.) Now, chez Yeung, a sweeping wall of glass defines the living room, nearly dead-on where Meyer envisioned the original boundary. Inside reside the couple's curated collections of fine Peking glass and rare Chinese pieces from the Tang, Han, and Qing dynasties—collections that play peacefully with Ka's own photography, Jan's spirited finds, and the superstars of Danish, Japanese, and French furniture design. This is precisely what can happen when two unlikely soul mates (he from Hong Kong, she from Iowa) find their groove and furnish their world—a world where we highly recommend the lychee martinis.

opposite "Good fortune," promises Jan and Ka Yeung's front door, painted by artist Charles Howard from Chinese characters digitally "stretched" by Ka Yeung. The lithograph above the Chinese herbal chest, *The Big Family No. 5,* is by Zhang Xiaogang. The pair of bowls is from the Qing dynasty.

preceding pages The slat-back rosewood sofa is Chinese, from the 1960s; the rosewood coffee table is nineteenth-century Chinese. The rug is Odegard. At far right is a handmade bench by Mira Nakashima, daughter of designer George Nakashima. The Papa Bear chairs are by Hans Wegner. In the back corner is one of a pair of rare British-made Quad 57 electrostatic speakers with their original metal grilles. Against the glass wall is a luxuriously long George Nakashima table. *above* In the dining room, a Hans Wegner buffet holds part of the Yeungs' collection of Peking glass. The back wall is an eye-popping gallery of photography's greats. The table is Le Corbusier. *below* The painting—measuring a monumental eight by ten feet—is a self-portrait by Zhang Fazhi.

above left The pair of honeycomb vases spouting fresh pomegranates is nineteenth-century Peking glass, as is the bowl between them, prized for its double-fused design and motif of bats, a symbol of good luck in China. Ka replaced the Le Corbusier table's usual glass top with a wooden one, which he decoupaged with pages from Chinese almanacs. *above right* A pair of nineteenth-century blackwood chairs from South China sports pillows covered in Etro fabric. The tripod-leg table, circa 1950, is an early Knoll offering by Swiss designer Hans Bellman. The bookcase by Kurt Østevig holds everything from a Peking-glass fish to a Tibetan "singing bowl," made of seven metals. At far right is a limited-edition Eames rosewood screen. *left* A Hans Wegner table and chairs are watched over by Philippe Halsman's iconic photomontage of Mao Tse-tung and Marilyn Monroe, made in the 1950s at the request of Salvador Dalí. "Some people," Jan says, "have asked if that's Ka in drag!" At far left are Chinese revolutionary figures.

KIMBERLY AND JUSTIN WHITMAN

Welcome to the high-rise apartment of your movie dreams, a cinematic place that decorator Jan Showers has propped with French furnishings from the 1940s and modern art—the perfect backdrop for a young couple's cinematic life together. Only this is no movie.

Put down your popcorn: Kimberly Schlegel Whitman and husband Justin Whitman are living real life here, high above a posh and leafy city boulevard. It's a picture-perfect pad, with a double-door entry; a dark, dramatic foyer; and a sweeping, side-to-side great room staged with a baby-grand piano, a dangly capiz-shell chandelier, and all manner of glamour. Oh, and the view: floor-to-ceiling glass walls framing a panoramic vista over a Frank Lloyd Wright–designed theater building, across the avenue to other glittering high-rises and as far north as the eye can see. This is one Tinseltown-ready tale, filmed in CinemaScope, Panavision, the works—a terribly swish place that *The Thin Man*'s elegant Nick and Nora Charles would have loved .

High-rise living suits the Whitmans just fine, thank you. When husband Justin, the son of movie actor Stuart Whitman, even hints at maybe finding a nice little house, his wife tells him, "I am *not* moving out of here unless you can supply three valets, a concierge, and a doorman!" It was, you see, her bachelorette pad first. After signing the deed on this 2,400-square-foot apartment, the future Mrs. Whitman called on Showers to set the stage for an already busy life. But first, a little editing. The 1980s built-ins and burgundy marble: *Cut!* Pared-down surfaces and reconfigured rooms: *Action!* With a freshened kitchen, a bedroom converted to an office, and an enlarged entry hall, Showers and Whitman turned DeMille and Dietrich, working together to infuse the place with a mix of new and old, French and American, pink and mink. "It's hilarious," says Showers, who collaborated with Schlegel on a previous home, "Kim and I know what each other is going to say."

The production was a smash, and now the Whitmans have a glam-couple lair to go with their glam-couple lives. But, truth be told, this is no Hollywood soundstage: It really is a functioning, fun place where the cell phone twitters, the good dog Lola yaps, the housekeeper whisks about, and those double doors swing open frequently, with walk-ons by The Hair Colorist, The Delivery Man, The Mothers-In-Law, even The Decorator. But if you squint just so, you can almost see Nick and Nora over by that cart of Bombay gin, slouched on a French '40s divan against that VistaVision city view, slinging their trademark barbs and having a very swell time.

opposite The entry hall features a 1940s Andre Arbus commode, a pink Venetian-glass lamp, and a painting by Peter Jordan, all under a 1920s Venetian-glass chandelier found in Paris.

preceding pages The main salon features an unusual, vintage A. Bord piano from France, a Jan Showers–designed Parsons table and sofa; a pair of hand-gilded porcelain "trophy" lamps found in New York and reshaded; Louis-style, brown-leather chairs. *opposite* Custom purple-silk pillows adorn a Jan Showers–designed banquette in ironed and waxed leather. The modern-classic Lucite floor lamps are by Hinson. The gilded-iron cocktail table was found in Paris, as was the ebonized and mirrored bar cabinet at right. The framed woven-paper work is by artist Rusty Scruby. *above* The home office features a show-stopper of a mirrored desk. The acrylic-and-wood desk lamp is 1960s; the 1950s French chairs are newly ebonized and upholstered in vanilla leather. The curtains are chocolate taffeta.

SISTIE AND HENRY STOLLENWERCK

No pair of stone lions here. No, what greets you as you approach this "tree house" nestled on a wooded corner lot is instead a stone boar. That's right, a boar. With his own spotlight trained on him. Marlin Perkins would have loved it here. Take one step into the sheer-glass entry vestibule sandwiched between two massive stone walls, and things get even wilder. Look right: A stuffed dik-dik leaps across a windowpane. Look left: A leopard springs off a second-story catwalk. (You can almost imagine him landing paws first onto something rare and antique and Chinese in the living room below.) Further inspection reveals some telling books on the shelves: *Predators. Great Cats. Everest.* Goes well with the David Bates sculpture, the Mark Flood lace painting, and tomes on Steuben glass, Billy Baldwin, and Rolls-Royces.

And already we have exposed the secret of the Stollenwerck house: It is one of the most highly individual homes known to man. Or beast. Architect Gary Cunningham has probably never forgotten the day Sistie Stollenwerck—wife, mother, philanthropist, big-game hunter—called. Forty-plus years in a "soft contemporary" had run its course: The Stollenwercks were ready for a change. "I told him I wanted a tree house," she says, and thus began a spirited collaboration between, as Sistie puts it, "a talented architect who's not threatened by his client's vision—that's rare" and a woman with, well, a decidedly strong vision. Up went thick Pennsylvania blue-limestone walls, concrete floors, acres of glass, walnut ceilings held aloft by beautifully bowed pine beams, and warm copper trim. A pixilated pattern of multicolored shingles was wrapped around the second-story "box" that is the master suite. Every material here is expressed honestly, shown for what it is. Window frames are left unstained. The ceiling's steel plates and bolts are exposed. There is no hiding.

Sitting at the dining-room table, curled-up taxidermy lion just visible over her shoulder, Sistie recounts how she set about furnishing her tree house with favorite pieces—freshened up and rethought with the help of decorator Neal Stewart—from her previous house. Family heirlooms, blackamoors, a 1930s birdcage here, a pair of French chairs there—it is an electrifying contrast of fanciful furniture, wild animals, and gutsy, contemporary artworks. But it doesn't take long for the conversation to drift back to her beloved trips and safaris and, this time, gorillas. She claps her hands together in a sharp crack. "Did I tell you I'm going to Rwanda? I am. To see the gorilla nests. You can hike right up and get very close." She laughs her deep, unmistakable Sistie laugh. "That's my next project, even if it's my finale."

opposite On the catwalk, a prize leopard, bagged by Sistie, takes flight over the great room. The antique sofa on the far wall belonged to Sistie's mother. The ribbonlike painting high over the sofa is by Charles Aberg.

opposite page The vista from the great room, through the light-filled entry vestibule and into the library. The walls are stacked pieces of blue limestone left over from cutting larger pieces for other walls in the house. The fixture in the vestibule is a church lantern from Italy, hung upside down to better fit the space. The mounted Cape-buffalo skull carries a small brass plaque reading "Sistie. Tanzania—1992." ***above*** A screen of spears and kudu antelope horns— drilled and secured into the hundred-year-old, ebonized-pine floor and tied with humble twine— shields the house's one-and-only bedroom. On the wall are an African feather hat, an early David Bates painting, and a pair of coach lights from the front of the Stollenwercks' previous house. ***left*** Sistie spotted this collection of German Meissen porcelain leopards —complete with Victorian antique furniture — in an antiques showroom. "I fainted over them!" she says. Then she lowers her voice. "Then I found out the price and fainted again." The beaded African chair was found in Santa Fe, New Mexico; the elephant is one of a pair of rare betel-nut boxes, converted into lamps.

opposite above Guess who's coming to dinner. Under a Mark Flood lace painting is the king of the jungle, bagged by Henry Stollenwerck. The sheer solidity of the thick, Pennsylvania blue-limestone walls is evident here: The feeling is of being well protected inside a modernist castle. *opposite below* The library is wildly intellectual, its shelves filled with books on everything from Winston Churchill to Australia. The painting of books—hung wittily in front of the real books—is by artist Bill Davenport. Leaping over the whole tableau is a dik-dik, a tiny antelope, upper right, brought back from a night hunt in Africa. *above* In the trophy room, a Jeff Elrod digital painting is ringed by souvenirs of safaris gone by, including a warthog and a buffalo. The gazelles carry brass plaques that read "Taken by Sistie Stollenwerck." The column-base dining table, surrounded by classic McGuire leather director's chairs, is topped with re-cycled wood flooring from the couple's previous house. The Cubist chicken vessel on the table is by French sculptor Claude Lalanne. *left* The two-story fireplace is made of—prepare yourself—fossilized worms. Eerily beautiful, the stone comes from the small town of Lueders, Texas.

CHRISTOPHER RIDOLFI

It just had to be a high-rise. When decorator Christopher Ridolfi went hunting for new digs for his most finicky client—himself—he felt a pull toward living high in the sky. Perhaps it was a reaction to his previous residence, a one-story, ground-hugging suburban ranch. Maybe it was a little Pavlovian conditioning: The Boston-born Ridolfi grew up in a brownstone and was drawn to skyscraper life because, he says, "I had been accustomed to stepping out the front door and seeing people, street activity, and tall buildings." Whatever the case, he found his haven, here in a high-rise by celebrated modernist Howard Meyer, where the ingenious pinwheel arrangement of the building's footprint means that every apartment gets maximum glazing and light. At night, views of a glittery city—sparkling vistas, of course, are key to the urbane lifestyle—twinkle through the building's trademark see-through sunscreens, made of concrete and recalling the geometry of Piet Mondrian.

Inside Ridolfi's lair, things are just as artful. The decorator limits the overall colors of the apartment to a blend of taupes, beiges, and chocolates. Honeyed golds add just enough sheen; nothing jars, nothing jangles. Ridolfi was lucky to inherit the cozy, pecky-cypress walls from the previous owner: They add an organic element to an interior that might have tilted a little too hardcore midcentury mod. The herringbone-patterned teak floors? He inherited those, too. Ridolfi simply had them hand-waxed to preserve the years of patina and character. (A gentleman knows not to obliterate the past, but to build on it.) With a warm, elegant shell in place, Ridolfi folded in his favorite pieces, stirring and mixing to create some rather sophisticated juxtapositions. In the living room, he combines a chunky, angular sofa inspired by Jean-Michel Frank with a light and airy 1960s cocktail table that he found at a Paris flea market. (International travel: essential to the high-rise life.) Ridolfi hung contemporary art on the traditionally paneled walls and created even more contrasts in mood and materials. One example: the raised texture of faux-crocodile wallpaper in the entry hall, playing off a finely drawn wood commode attributed to Andre Arbus, which in turn holds a shimmery Belgian-glass lamp and a pair of burnished walrus tusks mounted on gleaming Lucite. A FontanaArte mirror from the 1930s presides over all—just the thing for checking one's appearance when dashing out the door to dinner, drinks, the opera, or a show. Or, if staying in, Ridolfi has only to whoosh open the glass wall in his bedroom and step out onto his cinematic terrace propped with all the necessary fittings: plump seating and plenty of cocktail tables for cigarettes and Scotches, whether it's a party for one, two, or twenty-two.

opposite The unmistakable concrete window screens—called brise soleil—of Christopher Ridolfi's 1957 high-rise, one of Dallas's landmark residential buildings, by architect Howard Meyer. In the living room are a travertine-topped English console table with pen-work finish, a Directoire-style chair, and a custom X-leg bench designed by Ridolfi.

opposite In one corner of the capacious living room, Ridolfi combines a white-leather 1950s chair by Italian designer Marco Zanuso with an American teak-and-slate side table and an Italian lamp, both from the 1960s and both from his parents. The birds on the bookshelf are Japanese porcelain bisque; the looping Lucite candlestick is by Dorothy Thorpe. *above* The entry hall showcases faux-crocodile wallpaper, a wood commode attributed to André Arbus, a Val Saint-Lambert lamp of Belgian glass, and a contemporary blown-glass vase by Vanessa Mitrani. A FontanaArte mirror from the 1930s presides over the tableau. The carved-wood chair is Guatemalan; the living room's walls and bookcases are pecky cypress. *right* In the master bedroom, the button-tufted linen bed is Ridolfi's own design. The bedcover is an antique suzani textile from Uzbekistan. The burled-walnut Louis-Philippe chest from the 1800s holds an Austrian Arts and Crafts lamp. Over the bed hangs Ridolfi's own work, in oil stick on canvas board. *following pages* On Ridolfi's cinematic terrace, the Mondrian-esque brise soleil filters the sun's rays—a changing light show every day.

how you look at it

JOHN BOBBITT

If you squint just so, you could be in a flat in the West Village. Or perhaps tucked away in one of the more charming *arrondissements* of Paris. But in fact, once your vision sharpens, you're standing squarely inside decorator John Bobbitt's cozy apartment, in one of Dallas' landmark old buildings, all Mediterranean and tile-roofed, with cage-door elevators and that delicious, delicious smell that only comes from decades' worth of paste wax and oil soap. Indeed, this particular residence within the 1920s-era dwelling has all the right cues: a thick entry door with chunky locks; a long hall that urges you forward into a gracious living room; even a teeny, tiny kitchen with the requisite black-and-white checkerboard floor. It's an enticing warren of little rooms, with deep woodwork, plaster ceilings, and stories to tell.

Which is precisely where Bobbitt comes in. This apartment, you see, has found its perfect inhabitant—world traveler, bon vivant, consummate storyteller. "Did I tell you about that chandelier?" he asks, gesturing to the silver stunner that dangles over his rosewood dining table. His eyes start to narrow and twinkle. "Bought it at a Paris flea. Didn't want to wait three months for it to get home. Well, it comes apart in about sixty pieces, you see, so I asked the hotel concierge for a screwdriver…" You can guess the rest: The late-nineteenth-century silver-gilt chandelier came home in Bobbitt's suitcase. And so it goes, with the antique clock drive that Bobbitt topped with glass and uses as a coffee table ("There's still a crank. You can really get it going"), with the little taxidermy bird on a table ("I bought it, forgetting that I would have to go through customs"), even with the Davenport desk in the library ("My grandfather used to keep one by his bed. He'd get up and write down his thoughts and dreams"). History, family, travels, rare engravings—Bobbitt loves it all. His books are well-thumbed, proffering tales of Cairo, jungles, Scottish houses, and Edgar Allan Poe. And here, in his own digs, he'll happily point out the howdah cushion that was once used for riding elephants or the tufted sofa that he rescued from a shop just before its faded red leather was about to be dyed fresh black. (Bobbitt recoils in horror at the idea.) In fact, so rooted in history and lore are all his collected things that only two shots of modernity reveal themselves: a chrome-and-glass side table designed by Eileen Gray and a little metal model of an F-86 Sabre fighter jet. Fix another martini and settle in: Bobbitt's got a story about that last one, too.

opposite The dining room features a William IV tilt-top table of rosewood, which decorator John Bobbitt rebuilt after someone else's unfortunate conversion to a coffee table. Overhead is a late-nineteenth-century silver-gilt bronze chandelier, which Bobbitt brought home from Paris in pieces in his luggage. The hand-colored engravings are by William Alexander.

opposite In the living room is a pair of slouchy club chairs, designed by Bobbitt, and an antique camel-hair carpet. The green chair at far left was found on a street in New York, tossed out as garbage. Bobbitt had it reworked in sumptuous Rubelli velvet. The coffee table is a glass-topped antique clockwork, complete with bell chime. **above** Tusks and objets are arranged in an artful assemblage. **below** Bobbitt installed a pair of antique doors between the apartment's tiny kitchen and cozy dining room.

opposite The library is off the living room. Overhead is a breathtaking Fortuny lamp—"this is the biggest"— which Bobbitt keeps hitched close to the ceiling; it would almost fill the room if untied. The daybed, in gorgeously patinated walnut and covered in a Persian carpet, is late-eighteenth-century/early-nineteenth-century French. The glass-and-wood table is an antique Japanese doll box; Bobbitt displays a pair of ceremonial men's shoes—size eleven, Bobbitt confirms, "and they do fit me"— inside the base. The red-leather wing-back chair is a flea-market find; next to it is an English Davenport desk like the one Bobbitt's grandfather kept at his bedside. Over the desk hangs a boxed moth collection from the 1940s and '50s. **above** A pair of miniature Vienna bronzes—monkeys gone fishing—and a taxidermy bird that Bobbitt found at a Paris flea market. **above right** Under a hand-colored, eighteenth-century engraving of a French port scene are a neoclassical urn of solid Carrara marble and a late-nineteenth-century illustration of Cupid riding a skull, alongside the handwritten Charles Baudelaire poem "L'Amour et le Crâne." **right** A bronze sculpture of a crying baby (its provenance unknown) is displayed on a teak-and-ivory chess set that Bobbitt's grandmother brought back from Hawaii in the late 1950s or early '60s.

MICKEY ROSMARIN

This rock-and-roll story starts with Biba in London and ends, in a whirlwind of fashion, at an imposing Mediterranean house with an eccentric bent. Mickey Rosmarin—owner of the iconic women's fashion emporium Tootsies in Houston, Dallas, and Atlanta, and inhabitant of this old-world, in-town villa—looks back to the 1970s when it all began. The inspiration for his store was a sensation happening on the other side of the pond: the boutique Biba in London. "I think Biba opened the same year we did, 1974," Rosmarin says. "It was fun and fresh, and was a complete inspiration. I even have the first catalog they ever made." Rosmarin sped from New York to Paris, Miami to St. Barth's and St. Tropez, picking up ideas and inspiration for his stores, as well as furnishings and art for his home. In the '80s, it wasn't a Saturday night unless there was a party at his store with visiting designers such as Donna Karan, Robert Lee Morris, Zandra Rhodes, Paloma Picasso, Michael Kors, and Diane von Furstenberg dropping by.

His magnificent, rambling, 1920s-era house, designed by William Ward Watkins, provides suitably surreal surroundings for his cache of prime modernist treasures by Eileen Gray, Gilbert Rohde, Edwin Lutyens, Karl Springer and more (which Rosmarin snapped up in Miami and L.A. and stowed away for decades), as well as his collections of Art Deco and Italian modern furnishings from the '40s and '50s. Also in residence are Hollywood Regency blackamoors from an estate in New Orleans, a *verre églomisé* from a Louisiana motel, Edwin Lutyens chairs designed for The Gleneagles Hotel in Scotland, black velvet Moderne sofas from an old Miami hotel, and bits of wild-animal prints and glints of gold. The house offers its own eccentricities: There are hidden-away telephone rooms, a secret chamber in the library reached by clicking a lock behind the bookshelves, even a maze in the gardens. Art ranges from vivid and surreal Donald Roller Wilson paintings to provocative Cindy Sherman black-and-white photographs, a series of Mexican pastel portraits from the '40s and Rachel Hecker's portrait of Montgomery Clift. Designer Richard Holley was called in to help make sense of the vast storerooms of furnishings. "What I do want to tell you, if I tell you nothing else of what I know about Mickey Rosmarin," Holley says, "is that he has never, ever varied or swayed from a point of view. His vision is crystal clear."

Cooling his jets and spending more time rooted at home these days with a tweenager and two dogs, Rosmarin surfs eBay for collectibles and finds himself on the receiving end of calls from antiques dealers whenever something fetching crosses their paths. After all, they know spot-on his Miami-meets-Paris-Moderne taste.

opposite The sepia-toned photograph of Hawaii is one of Mickey Rosmarin's most treasured possessions. The rosewood buffet, one of a pair with carved-gilt detailing, was made in Italy in the Art Deco style. The dining table and chairs are late 1940s Italian.

opposite The Art Deco–style table holds the mixings
for cocktails. Tufted, velvet-covered, '50s modern
chairs were bought from a Miami dealer on eBay.
Murano glass lamps. The painted screens were
bought in the 1970s. *above* In Rosmarin's sym-
metrically arranged living room is a pair of black
Moderne velvet-upholstered sofas acquired from an
old Miami hotel. In foreground, Edwin Lutyens chairs
designed for the Gleneagles resort in Scotland,
along with the *verre églomisé* from a Louisiana motel
that hangs above the fireplace. Mies van der Rohe
chaise longue. The bent-glass table was created
in the 1930s. *right* In the living room, artist Rachel
Hecker's portrait of Montgomery Clift hangs above a
Hollywood Regency commode. The hoof-and-clove
stool is Italian. *following pages* Architect William
Ward Watkins' graciously curved staircase in the
entry of the 1923 Mediterranean-style house. The
center table with a harp-shaped base, like the black-
and-taupe striped, upholstered bench, has rotated
from house to house for decades.

CHARLES ROSEKRANS and JON GREEN

Breeze through the iron garden gate, past the manicured boxwood hedges, and up the stairs to the exuberant Zuber-wallpapered foyer of this 1920s-era house, and you may hear the melodic sounds of Charles Rosekrans hard at work behind his Bösendorfer. A former conductor of the Houston Grand Opera, Rosekrans now travels the world conducting, playing, and recording classical music. When in residence, though, not a day goes by that you won't find him passionately playing his concert grand piano for hours on end, the music wafting through deliciously offbeat rooms with a wide-ranging scale of antique and modern, murals and painted papers, pagodas and chinoiserie.

Sharing the rambling space is Rosekrans's friend, decorator Jon Green, who took on this personal project and envisioned an interior worlds away from the one he discovered when Rosekrans acquired the house in 1972. A holiday Green spent in Stockholm and Denmark helped drive the design. "I was struck by the old-world backgrounds, layered with contemporary furnishings," he says, "so I decided in every room I was going to add a modern piece that really didn't belong in the setting—like the Saarinen table in the breakfast room and the Christian Eckart painting in the dining room. It needed a little modern freshness added without changing the architecture and the feeling of the house." Green was also inspired by the cinematic, over-the-top Venetian palazzos designed by the late decorator and set designer Tony Duquette for Rosekrans's sister-in-law and late brother, Dodie and John Rosekrans from San Francisco. Duquette's exotica—shell-encrusted furnishings, layered palettes of color and pattern, fringes, murals, antlers, and ephemera—is a feisty match for Green's metronome-precise eye for color, pattern, and unexpected juxtaposition.

The Italianate house, just two doors down from the brick Georgian house in which the legendary Howard Hughes grew up, has been reconfigured to stately proportions with a four-story pool house with guest quarters, poolside cabana, bath and sauna, home gym, a stately greenhouse for an orchard of orange and lemon trees, and, most importantly, a stunning music room. Green and Rosekrans hold twice-yearly soirées for fifty honored guests, intimate concerts with string and horn players accompanying Rosekrans' mighty grand piano.

opposite In the living room, the black-painted Regency sofa is from Minton-Spidell and is covered in Travers damask; the cocktail table is French eighteenth-century. A pair of Gainsborough chairs is covered in crewelwork from Chelsea Editions.

opposite In the upstairs hallway, a milk-painted black highboy, made in Pennsylvania, displays a collection of blue-and-white delft and Chinese jars. The framed prints of American Indian chiefs are by McKenney & Hall, from a series commissioned by the Smithsonian. **above** A gentleman's closet. **below** In a bedroom, a lampshade by VHH Designs has an Italian landscape printed on watercolor paper. The scrolled headboard design is based on a traditional colonial New England style usually crafted from maple. For reasons of comfort, Green covered it in Bennison fabric instead.

opposite Green covered the floor in the Scandinavian-inspired breakfast room and kitchen area with a black-and-white diamond pattern of porcelain. The blue-and-white antique china in the pair of ebony-painted corner cupboards is Worcester, circa 1850. The framed wallpaper remnant, salvaged from the recent remodel was the home's original dining room covering. The Gustavian-style chairs are painted. The fabric on the banquette is by Manuel Canovas. *above left* The drinks bar in the dining room was created out of a commode of Green's own design. Laminated with Fortuny fabric and trimmed with French brass details, it features a mirrored top and is filled with Georgian glass decanters and bar accoutrements, including a vintage silver Mexican tequila decanter. The oil painting is from an antiques shop in Vienna. *above right* In the dining room, an eighteenth-century French gilt mirror reflects a Christian Eckart work, *Whitpainting*. An eighteenth-century Queen Anne mahogany drop-leaf table is topped with ollas from Uriarte Talavera in Puebla, Mexico, and a small collection of blanc de chine pagodas. The crystal chandelier is by Baccarat. The mural hand-painted by Jon Green depicts a Chinese trade scene and was inspired by a trip he took to Nantucket: He spied similar wallpaper hanging in a historical captain's home and remembered the look to recreate it. *left* The French parterre-inspired garden has a cozy conversation area with a sofa covered in Scalamandré's all-weather Neptune's Treasure and Philippe Starck chair. The lacquered temple table is a Chinese antique.

MIKYUNG CHUN

Something happens when the front doors chez Mikyung Chun swing open. Your brain knows you're in a gated suburban community, but your senses do a little shuffle. There is music: sultry and tribal. There is aroma: spicy and floral. And then there is Chun: a force field of energy and charm, decked in cutting-edge Chanel, coming to greet you.

Chun, proprietress of a tony modern-furniture showroom, has worked hard on her personal haven. Six years in the making, with a long pause while she returned to her native Korea, the house looks like no other in its neighborhood of earth-toned Tudors and conservative Georgians. Think blinding-white stucco; architectural cues that read Italian, Gothic, French, Bahamian; even a tile roof that is pure Chun—pure white, where traditional red or green tiles wouldn't do. On the property, the whiteout continues: A white stucco wall wraps its arms around the adjacent lot, which Chun bought from the outset and planted with cool, green grass. Behind the main house, things get more "resort" than "residential," with white canvas umbrellas, white awnings, and a sparkling pool shaped like the bow on a package. There are groups of Starck chairs for gabbing and small tables that Chun routinely sets with bottles of water, fresh roses, and linens—blinding white, of course.

Inside, the story changes. Sort of. Chun has deftly played white against black, soft against hard, old against new. Snow-white furniture pulsates on black marble. A gleaming white Saarinen tulip-base coffee table snuggles into a chocolate-colored Fendi fur rug. These moments of high contrast please Chun, who, for such a proponent of current, contemporary design, deliberately designed her house with traditional elements inside—deep woodwork, thickly troweled walls, plaster garlands—so that her fast-forward furnishings would resonate even more vividly. Not that she shuns the storied or the old: In her grand living room, a carved and gilded 1800s French piano plays off a chair designed only a decade ago. Upstairs, in her bedroom, an eighteenth-century bergère and ottoman sidle right up to a cigarette table that Chun designed herself. And everywhere, air and space and light swirl around the pieces, old and new, showing them to their best advantage. But make no mistake—this minimalist has a romantic side, and it has to do with her love of hotels. She speaks of Philippe Starck's surreal Delano Hotel in Miami and the Mondrian in Los Angeles; Grace Leo-Andrieu's charming Hotel Lancaster in Paris and the way Leo-Andrieu takes care of everyone; and a certain hotel she knows of in Austria, run by friends. It all starts to make sense. Here in her own home, she gets to check in—to the surreal life—every day.

opposite A marble-topped chess table designed by Mikyung Chun cozies up to the fireplace in the family room. The iron sculpture becomes the family tree over the holidays, hung with silver baubles and crystals.

opposite top Chun's airy aerie has just a few carefully chosen furnishings and one legendary lady. The photo enlargement on canvas of Sophia Loren was done for Chun in Italy. The two-door cabinet in the background is a prototype designed by Chun, and the white bergère and ottoman are antique Louis XIV, covered in Promemoria velvet. Philippe Starck's Vicieuse height-adjustable tables do bedside duty. **opposite bottom left** In a nook off the upstairs hallway, Starck's iconic '80s Costes chairs circle his Lord Yi table. **opposite bottom right** Dining table is from FreWil's "Geometrics" series, with chairs by Modénature and high-back chairs and a curved banquette designed by Chun. Chun also designed the silvered-glass armoire and assembled the chandelier from parts of other fixtures and had the whole concoction painted white. **left** A curvy sunken tub echoes the window and mirror. **below left** Chun couldn't find the perfect" table, so she designed her own from powder-coated iron and named it Ms. P. **below right** Chun found this elegant chair and had its original crisscrossed bars and center medallion removed from the back because she preferred "just the simple, oval shape."

CATHY ECHOLS

Relying on her unerring eye for all things fashionable, the Tom Ford–worshipping, Hermès-wearing Cathy Echols remodeled and decorated her own house with the same sense of unstudied coordination and cheeky irreverence. For many years, Echols and her former husband restored houses. "An outdated space is like a canvas," she says. "When you paint, you start with a raw canvas, and it presents itself to you, and you keep working on it and developing it. That's what I enjoy doing." The blank canvas before her, a 1979 gated town house where she currently resides, had only known one set of former owners—and they had taken full advantage of the colored porcelains, molded carpets, and vivid paint colors of the era. Echols brought the space up to date by replacing every colored plumbing fixture with simple white-and-chrome fixtures and changing out the carpets for the knottiest, lowest-grade maple planks she could find. "I love the texture," she says of the warm wood, which she finished with a matte whitewashed coating.

She elected to keep the deep, carved crown molding inside what could be called an architecturally hybrid home, the exterior of which features a mansard roof and mix of colonial elements. She asked her painter to create a Venetian plaster effect over the sheetrock inside to unify the first-floor living and dining areas, and to glaze the plaster a stormy shade of gray called Seine. The result: a sophisticated backdrop where antiques with a sense of history and cool, contemporary pieces could share company.

An avid cook, Echols outfitted the kitchen with a professional Wolf gas range; a large-scale double-faucet utility sink; and row and rows of deep, open shelves to display her vast collection—some pieces precious, some not—of white china. She replaced the typical center isle with a large butcher's-block table that doubles as a dining area and workstation, a space where you'll often find her son, thirteen-year-old Stuart, tackling homework or painting along with his mom.

Through the black swinging kitchen door is the bistro, a swank space where Echols entertains with frequent dinner parties and cozy tête-à-têtes. In both her bar with its undulating curved shelves and her low-lit bistro with plush mohair banquettes, Echols borrowed a page from the book of Charles James, the American couturier commissioned by Dominique de Menil to design her modernist home, his only interior-design project. "I think that Charles James was trying to do what I was trying to do: break up all the straight geometric lines," Echols says. And like James, Echols has effortless American style—a new brand of chic.

opposite The painting of a protective angel in Cathy Echols's bedroom was discovered on holiday in San Miguel de Allende. The chair is horn; the head on the steel-and-glass table is Indonesian.

Stick
it

COCKTAIL MENU

opposite In the dining room, also known as "the bistro," a Moorish lantern hangs above a voluminous pleated silk-taffeta skirt and a half-dozen Philippe Starck Louis Ghost chairs. Above the Victorian buffet is an oil painting by Robin Utterback, from Barbara Davis Gallery. *above* Echols created a deep red bar in an alcove. *below* In Echols's bedroom, burlap bolsters offset white linens. Echols created the oil-pastel-and-pencil portrait of her son Stuart on a map of Paris.

PAUL ROUAN
SAINT-CHINIAN
(HERAULT)

opposite In the living room is one of a pair of chocolate-leather armless chairs and a nail-head-accented sofa. The painting above the fireplace, by Pomm Jitpratuk, was found in Bangkok. **above** In the media room, an Alexander Calder print hangs above the leopard-spotted sectional. The cocktail table made with old piano legs and covered with a piece of slate was found at an estate sale. **below** A tiger-wood three-drawer commode and drawing by Rachel Hecker on an easel.

ANONYMOUS

It took a dream team of like-minded souls to make designer Michael Landrum's most curious of architectural visions—a ruin of a house perched at the edge of a bayou—a reality.

The house was commissioned by the kind of client most architects and designers pray will come their way: one willing to purge every belonging from a former existence. Landrum brought together a dream team of co-creators: the artist Michael Tracy, who fashioned furniture and rugs for the space; the interior designers Marcia Bland Brown of San Miguel de Allende and Gwynn Griffith of San Antonio; and famed landscape architect Sarah Lake. "I think that's the ideal way to do it," Landrum says. "If someone commissions a new house without preconceived notions or collections, it's nice to get as many like-minded people involved in the project as possible. It makes for a more interesting house."

Landrum's gestalt arose from a foundation of imposing limestone with a matrix of crystal at its core, which was quarried outside the small town of Georgetown, north of Austin, Texas. The burnt ochre–colored stone—its dust was crushed and mixed into the mortar to create indistinguishable seams between the mighty pieces—is integral to the house. "My thought was to create this idea of a found ruin, the sort of colonial structure you'd find in a Mexican border town," Landrum says. "It's an amalgam. It's not Spanish colonial, and it's not a gringo-type dwelling. It's closer to a native structure built by ranch workers long ago, where you've gone in and not really cleaned it up but left it intact and installed contemporary metal windows."

The house is theatrical—almost like a space the late Tony Duquette would have brainstormed, had he lived in Mexico. The design team custom-made much of the hacienda-style furniture and hand-made light fixtures in Brown's San Miguel de Allende workshop. Near the end of their three-year alliance—the critical stage when all the moving parts finally came together—Landrum hired the artist Michael Tracy to broaden the look of the house. "I felt Michael would be the perfect fit, because a lot of his earlier work, and to a certain extent a lot of his current work, is derived from Mexico and that sort of pageantry and theater of Catholicism and the New World," Landrum says. "I wanted to get a little bit of sleekness into the overall composition, and his furniture is derived from a Luis Barragán aesthetic. There is a crudeness about it, but also a sophistication that would really make the house pop." Some of Tracy's woven rugs are saturated with pure color, such as the vibrant violet piece in the living room; others incorporate designs derivative of his artwork, while the Tracy-designed furniture is rustic, almost brutalist-looking, and pairs well with paintings by his protégé, Alejandro Diaz. With a compelling sense of tension that only this kind of dream team can evoke, the house makes a bold and rugged statement.

opposite A cantilevered, concrete, spiral staircase winds up to the second-floor study, which overlooks the living room. The cowhide-and-suede sofas are by Marcia Bland Brown. The Mexican bougainvillea-colored rug is designed by Michael Tracy. The armchairs are early–nineteenth-century French.

opposite right The rose-colored *traje de Luces* (matador's suit) from Spain, which stands in a niche in the entry hall, was an eBay acquisition. **opposite far right** The grid-wood armchair is one of a pair designed by Michael Tracy. The bronze candelabra is another of Tracy's designs. **opposite bottom right** Antique beams form the ceiling of the entry hall. A seventeenth-century Mexican painting of Nuestra Señora de Soledad. The front door is a set of antique Mexican *portones* from a seventeenth-century hacienda outside Queretaro. **opposite bottom far right** Intended to look like a structure native to the arid, rural landscape of South Texas, the exterior is fashioned from Texas-quarried limestone in a scale not usually attempted for residential applications. The San Antonio landscape designer Sarah Lake created the chiseled grid on the pavers to reinforce the rugged exterior. **left** A work on canvas by Alejandro Diaz looms above a collection of silver mercury balls on an overscale credenza by Marcia Bland Brown. **below left** At the touch of a button, the carved Mexican chest opens to reveal a flat-screen television. The Spanish baroque gilded bed is a copy of Bland Brown's own antique bed at her hacienda Calderone, outside San Miguel de Allende. **below** In the great living room, Michael Tracy's cowhide-covered sofa.

CREDITS

p. 8 Mike Thompson. Interiors designed by Mike Thompson. Produced and written by Rob Brinkley. Photography Ka Yeung. **p. 16 Dominique and John de Menil.** Architectural restoration William F. Stern and David Bucek of Stern and Bucek Architects. Original architecture Philip Johnson. Original interiors designed by Charles James. Produced and written by Laurann Claridge. Photography Tria Giovan. Black-and-white shot of de Menils Hickey-Robertson. **p. 26 Christian Eckart and Jill Davies.** Produced by Laurann Claridge. Written by Catherine D. Anspon. Photography Tria Giovan. **p. 30 Bonnie Purvis and Ralph Edward Purvis Jr.** Interiors designed by Michelle Nussbaumer. Produced and written by Rob Brinkley. Photography Stephen Karlisch. Flowers Chris Whanger at J & C Design. **p. 38 Lucy and Steve Wrubel.** Architecture Paul Jankowski, Zero3. Interiors designed by Lucy and Steve Wrubel, with Neal Stewart. Produced and written by Rob Brinkley. Photography Steve Wrubel. **p. 44 Michael Landrum and Philip Paratore.** Architectural renovation Michael T. Landrum Inc. Design consultant Gwen Griffith. Produced and written by Laurann Claridge. Photography Tria Giovan. **p. 50 Lisa Pope Westerman and Greg Westerman.** Architectural renovation and interiors designed by Lisa Pope Westerman. Produced and written by Laurann Claridge. Photography Tria Giovan. **p. 56 Hiram Butler.** Interiors designed by Hiram Butler. Produced and written by Laurann Claridge. Photography Tria Giovan. **p. 62 George Sellers.** Interiors designed by George Sellers. Produced and written by Rob Brinkley. Photography Ka Yeung. Monster photograph Adam Fish. **p. 68 James McInroe.** Interiors designed by James McInroe. Produced and written by Rob Brinkley. Photography Ka Yeung. Styling Jan Yeung. **p. 72 Ken Downing and Sam Saladino.** Interiors designed by Ken Downing and Sam Saladino. Produced and written by Rob Brinkley. Photography Ka Yeung. **p. 78 Aaron Rambo.** Interiors designed by Aaron Rambo. Produced and written by Laurann Claridge. Photography Jack Thompson. **p. 84 David Lackey.** Interiors designed by David Lackey and Russell Prince. Produced by J. Randall Powers. Written by Laurann Claridge. Photography Hickey-Robertson. **p. 90 Rob Dailey and Todd Fiscus.** Interiors designed by Rob Dailey and Todd Fiscus. Produced and written by Rob Brinkley. Photography Ka Yeung. Flowers Avant Garden. **p. 96 Lester Marks.** Interiors designed by Lester Marks and Russell Duesterhoft. Produced and written by Laurann Claridge. Photography Tria Giovan. **p. 102 Eric Prokesh.** Interiors designed by Eric Prokesh. Produced and written by David Feld. Photography Mali Azima and Mark Roach. **p. 108 Richard Holley.** Interiors designed by Richard Holley. Produced and written by Laurann Claridge. Photography Tria Giovan. **p. 114 McKay Otto and Keith Coffee.** Interiors designed by McKay Otto. Produced by J. Randall Powers. Written by Catherine D. Anspon. Photography Jack Thompson. **p. 120 Salle Werner-Vaughn.** Interiors designed by Salle Werner-Vaughn. Produced and written by Laurann Claridge. Photography Hickey-Robertson and Jack Thompson. **p. 126 Angie Barrett.** Interiors designed by James McInroe; guest bedroom by Jan Showers and James McInroe. Produced and written by Rob Brinkley. Photography Ka Yeung. Flowers Jeffrey Lee at Grange Hall/Urban Flower. **p. 132 Bill Mackin.** Interiors designed by Bill Mackin. Produced and written by Rob Brinkley. Photography Steve Wrubel. **p. 138 Rob Brinkley.** Interiors designed by Rob Brinkley. Produced and written by Rob Brinkley. Photography Steve Wrubel. **p. 144 Dana Harper.** Interiors designed by Dana Harper. Architectural restoration William F. Stern and David Bucek of Stern and Bucek Architects. Produced and written by Laurann Claridge. Photography Tria Giovan. **p. 150 Don Connelly.** Interiors designed by Don Connelly. Produced and written by Laurann Claridge. Photography Tria Giovan. Landscape design Brian Swallen. **p. 156 Kay O'Toole.** Interiors designed by Kay O'Toole. Produced and written by Laurann Claridge. Photography Hickey-Robertson. **p. 162 Lisa and King Grossman.** Interiors designed by J. Randall Powers. Architecture Allen Bianchi. Written by Laurann Claridge. Photography Tria Giovan. **p. 168 Amis and Guillaume Garrigue.** Interiors designed by Amis and Guillaume Garrigue. Architecture Bruce Goff. Produced and written by Rob Brinkley. Photography Guillaume Garrigue; exterior, hallway and bath photography Hickey-Robertson. **p. 174 Jan and Ka Yeung.** Interiors designed by Jan and Ka Yeung. Produced and written by Rob Brinkley. Photography Ka Yeung. Styling Jan Yeung. **p. 180 Kimberly and Justin Whitman.** Interiors designed by Jan Showers. Produced and written by Rob Brinkley. Photography Ka Yeung. Flowers Ron Schulz. **p. 186 Sistie and Henry Stollenwerck.** Interiors designed by Neal Stewart and Sistie Stollenwerck. Architecture Gary Cunningham. Produced and written by Rob Brinkley. Photography Ka Yeung. Styling Jan Yeung. **p. 192 Christopher Ridolfi.** Interiors designed by Christopher Ridolfi of William-Christopher Design. Produced and written by Rob Brinkley. Photography Ka Yeung. Flowers Jack Collins for Grange Hall/Urban Flower. **p. 198 John Bobbitt.** Interiors designed by John Bobbitt. Produced and written by Rob Brinkley. Photography Steve Wrubel. **p. 204 Mickey Rosmarin.** Interiors designed by Richard Holley. Produced and written by Laurann Claridge. Photography Tria Giovan. **p. 210 Charles Rosekrans and Jon Green.** Interiors designed by Jon Green. Written by Laurann Claridge. Photography Hickey-Robertson. **p. 216 Mikyung Chun.** Interiors designed by Mikyung Chun. Produced and written by Rob Brinkley. Photography Ka Yeung. **p. 220 Cathy Echols.** Interiors designed by Cathy Echols. Produced and written by Laurann Claridge. Photography Tria Giovan. **p. 226 Anonymous.** Architectural design Michael T. Landrum Inc. Furniture and rugs designed by Michael Tracy. Interiors designed by Marcia Bland Brown and Gwynn Griffith. Produced and written by Laurann Claridge. Photography Tria Giovan and Jack Thompson. Landscape design Sarah Lake.

ACKNOWLEDGMENTS

. . . or Whom We Couldn't Have Done It Without

Rob Brinkley, *PaperCity* magazine's design editor and Dallas co-editor, brings a distinguished vision and rapier wit to the pages of *PaperCity*—and to this book. He art-directed and wrote the narrative for 17 of the Dallas houses included herein. Houston features editor Laurann Claridge has a beautiful and knowledgeable writing voice, and she art-directed and wrote 17 of the Houston houses.

In The Beginning ...

Gratitude to Martine Assouline, with whom I had my first meeting in September 2007 (for which I was 10 minutes late, yet she was still lovely and gracious), and Prosper Assouline. Greg Fourticq Jr., a longtime *PaperCity* contributor who is now director of business development at Assouline. I've known him since . . . let's just say many years, and he's always inspired me. Our editor at Assouline, Esther Kremer, who has such vision, and Amy Trombat at Assouline, who has a magical eye for design. Diane Dorrans Saeks, a *PaperCity* contributor and author of 19 design books, who guided me through the beginning machinations of this book. Randy Powers, also a contributor, amazing decorator, and wonderful friend, who is an unflinching sounding board; and Becca Cason Thrash and Ken Downing, who expertly opined along the way.

Also the photographers who have contributed so mightily, in particular Ka Yeung in Dallas and his wife and stylist, Jan Yeung; they photographed 11 of the houses in this book. New York–based Tria Giovan, who flies to Houston to shoot for *PaperCity*; Tria photographed 13 houses in this book. Steve Wrubel, Stephen Karlisch and Guillaume Garrigue in Dallas; Jack Thompson, Paul Hester, and Blaine Hickey in Houston; and Mali Azima in Atlanta, who all photographed houses for the book. And I would like to thank Ogden Robertson, in memoriam, for his beautiful photographs of so many houses.

And there is Brooke Hortenstine, Dallas co-editor of *PaperCity*, whose own style quotient is off the charts. She held down the roost while we put this book together. Also, from *PaperCity*, Catherine D. Anspon for her art expertise, Ryland Peveto, Sharon L. Taylor for her eagle eye, Jenny Antill, Kate Allen Stukenberg, Meredith Riddle, Allie Fields, Monica Bickers, Margaret Stafford, Pam Winder, Chelsea Cunningham, Kayt Drickey, Mary Hoang, Jessica Johnson, Chad Miller, Kelli Roberts, Michelle Reid, James Work, Sarah Rufca, Bonnie Thompson, Shannon Crain, Dee Cleare, contributor Carol Isaak Barden, Bryan Deaktor, Will Logg, and the art department: Jessica Dunegan, Rebecca Saldaña, Kendra Juran, and Alfredo Figueroa. Richard Allison with Vertis Communications was instrumental in the color production of these photographs.

And a heartfelt thank you to my wonderful and supportive husband, Jim Kastleman, who is also the publisher of *PaperCity* magazine, and to our two children, Ben and Olivia Kastleman.

— Holly Moore Kastleman, May 2008